COMPUTER GRAPHICS

CG

K. GOKUL

Copyright © K. Gokul
All Rights Reserved.

Contents

CHAPTER ONE

Output Primitives

What is computer Graphics?

Computer graphics is an art of drawing pictures, lines, charts, etc. using computers with the help of programming. Computer graphics image is made up of number of pixels. Pixel is the smallest addressable graphical unit represented on the computer screen.

Introduction

? Computer is information processing machine. User needs to communicate with computer and the computer graphics is one of the most effective and commonly used ways of communication with the user.

? It displays the information in the form of graphical objects such as pictures, charts, diagram and graphs.

? Graphical objects convey more information in less time and easily understandable formats for example statically graph shown in stock exchange.

? In computer graphics picture or graphics objects are presented as a collection of discrete pixels.

? We can control intensity and color of pixel which decide how picture look like.

? The special procedure determines which pixel will provide the best approximation to the desired picture or graphics object this process is known as Rasterization.

? The process of representing continuous picture or graphics object as a collection of discrete pixels is called Scan Conversion.

Advantages of computer graphics

? Computer graphics is one of the most effective and commonly used ways of communication with computer.

? It provides tools for producing picture of "real-world" as well as synthetic objects such as mathematical surfaces in 4D and of data that have no inherent geometry such as survey result.

? It has ability to show moving pictures thus possible to produce animations with computer graphics.

? With the use of computer graphics we can control the animation by adjusting the speed, portion of picture in view the amount of detail shown and so on.

? It provides tools called motion dynamics. In which user can move objects as well as observes as per requirement for example walk throw made by builder to show flat interior and surrounding.

? It provides facility called update dynamics. With this we can change the shape color and other properties of object.

? Now in recent development of digital signal processing and audio synthesis chip the interactive graphics can now provide audio feedback along with the graphical feed backs.

Application of computer graphics

? User interface: - Visual object which we observe on screen which communicates with user is one of the most useful applications of the computer graphics.

? Plotting of graphics and chart in industry, business, government and educational organizations drawing like bars, pie-charts, histogram's are very useful for quick and good decision making.

? Office automation and desktop publishing: - It is used for creation and dissemination of information. It is used in in-house creation and printing of documents which contains text, tables, graphs and other formsof drawn or scanned images or picture.

? Computer aided drafting and design: - It uses graphics to design components and system such as automobile bodies structures of building etc.

? Simulation and animation: - Use of graphics in simulation makes mathematic models and mechanical systems more realistic and easy to study.

? Art and commerce: - There are many tools provided by graphics which allows used to make their picture animated and attracted which are used in advertising.

? Process control: - Now a day's automation is used which is graphically displayed on the screen.

? Cartography: - Computer graphics is also used to represent geographic maps, weather maps, oceanographic charts etc.

? Education and training: - Computer graphics can be used to generate models of physical, financial and economic systems. These models can be used as educational aids.

? Image processing: - It is used to process image by changing property of the image.

Display devices

? Display devices are also known as output devices.

? Most commonly used output device in a graphics system is a video monitor.

Cathode-ray-tubes

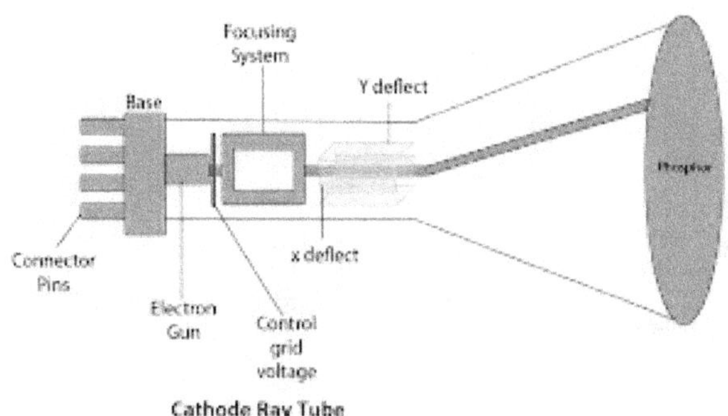

Cathode Ray Tube

? It is an evacuated glass tube.

? An electron gun at the rear of the tube produce a beam of electrons which is directed towards the screen of the tube by a high voltage typically 15000 to 20000 volts

? Inner side screen is coated with phosphor substance which gives light when it is stroked bye electrons.

? Control grid controls velocity of electrons before they hit the phosphor.

? The control grid voltage determines how many electrons are actually in the electron beam. The negative the control voltage is the fewer the electrons that pass through the grid.

? Thus control grid controls Intensity of the spot where beam strikes the screen.

? The focusing system concentrates the electron beam so it converges to small point when hits the phosphor coating.

? Deflection system directs beam which decides the point where beam strikes the screen.

Voltage applied to vertical and horizontal deflection plates is control vertical and horizontal deflection respectively.

? There are two techniques used for producing images on the CRT screen:

1. Vector scan/Random scan display.

2. Raster scan display.

Vector scan/Random scan display

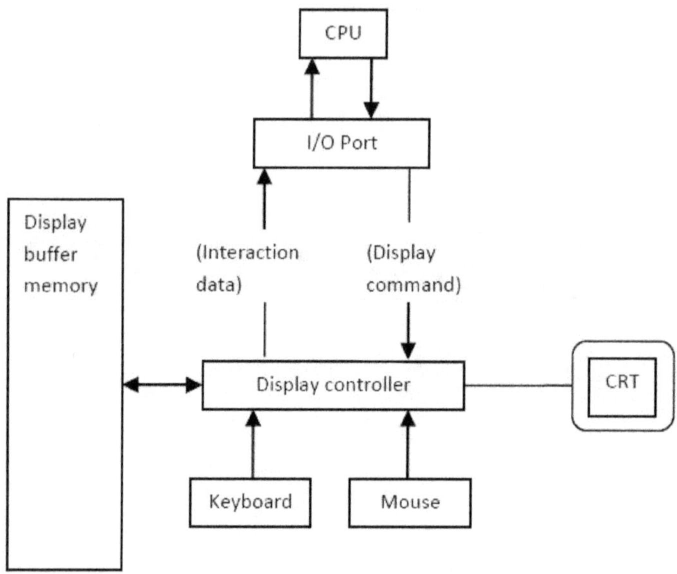

? Vector scan display directly traces out only the desired lines on CRT.

? If we want line between point p1 & p2 then we directly drive the beam deflection circuitry which focus beam directly from point p1 to p2.

? If we do not want to display line from p1 to p2 and just move then we can blank the beam as we move it.

? To move the beam across the CRT, the information about both magnitude and direction is required. This information is generated with the help of vector graphics generator.

? Fig. 1.2 shows architecture of vector display. It consists of display controller, CPU, display buffer memory and CRT.

? Display controller is connected as an I/O peripheral to the CPU.

? Display buffer stores computer produced display list or display program.

? The Program contains point & line plotting commands with end point co-ordinates as well as character plotting commands.

? Display controller interprets command and sends digital and point co-ordinates to a vector generator.

? Vector generator then converts the digital co-ordinate value to analog voltages for beam deflection circuits that displace an electron beam which points on the CRT's screen.

? In this technique beam is deflected from end point to end point hence this techniques is also called random scan.

? We know as beam strikes phosphors coated screen it emits light but that light decays after few milliseconds and therefore it is necessary to repeat through the display list to refresh the screen at least 30 times per second to avoid flicker.

? As display buffer is used to store display list and used to refreshing, it is also called refresh buffer.

Raster scan display.

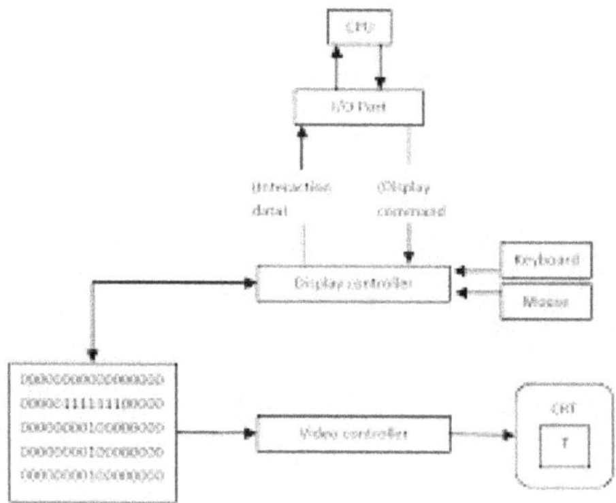

? It consists of display controller, CPU, video controller, refresh buffer, keyboard, mouse and CRT.

? The display image is stored in the form of 1's and 0's in the refresh buffer.

? The video controller reads this refresh buffer and produces the actual image on screen.

? It will scan one line at a time from top to bottom & then back to the top.

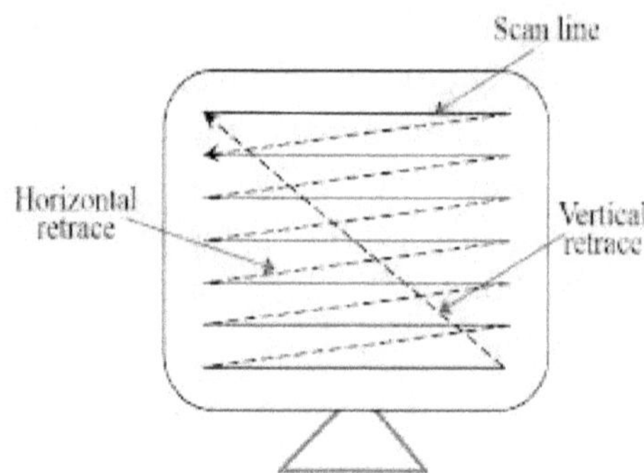

? In this method the horizontal and vertical deflection signals are generated to move the beam all over the screen

? Here beam is swept back & forth from left to the right.

? When beam is moved from left to right it is ON.

? When beam is moved from right to left it is OFF and process of moving beam from right to left after completion of row is known as Horizontal Retrace.

? When beam is reach at the bottom of the screen. It is made OFF and rapidly retraced back to the top left to start again and process of moving back to top is known as Vertical Retrace.

? The screen image is maintained by repeatedly scanning the same image. This process is known as

Refreshing of Screen.

? In raster scan displays a special area of memory is dedicated to graphics only. This memory is called

Frame Buffer.

? Frame buffer holds set of intensity values for all the screen points.

? That intensity is retrieved from frame buffer and display on screen one row at a time.

? Each screen point referred as pixel or Pel (Picture Element).

? Each pixel can be specified by its row and column numbers.

? It can be simply black and white system or color system.

? In simple black and white system each pixel is either ON or OFF, so only one bit per pixel is needed.

? Additional bits are required when color and intensity variations can be displayed up to 24-bits per pixel are included in high quality display systems.

? On a black and white system with one bit per pixel the frame buffer is commonly called a Bitmap. And for systems with multiple bits per pixel, the frame buffer is often referred as a Pixmap.

Difference between random scan and raster scan

	Vector Scan Display		Raster Scan Display
1.	In vector scan display the beam is moved between the end points of the graphics primitives.	1.	In raster scan display the beam is moved all over the screen one scan line at a time, from top bottom and then back to top.
2.	Vector display flickers when the number of primitives in the buffer becomes too large.	2.	In raster display, the refresh process is independent of the complexity of the image.
3.	Scan conversion is not required.	3.	Graphics primitives are specified in terms of their endpoints and must be scan converted into their corresponding pixels in the frame buffer.
4.	Scan conversion hardware is not required.	4.	Because each primitive must be scan-converted, real time dynamics is for more computational and requires separate scan conversion hardware.
5.	Vector display draws a continuous and smooth lines.	5.	Raster display can display mathematically smooth lines, polygons, and boundaries of curved primitives only by approximating them with pixels on the raster grid.
6.	Cost is more.	6.	Cost is low.
7.	Vector display only draws lines and characters.	7.	Raster display has ability to display areas filled with solid colours or patterns.

Output Primitives:

Points and Lines

? Point plotting is done by converting a single coordinate position furnished by an application program into appropriate operations for the output device in use.

? Line drawing is done by calculating intermediate positions along the line path between two specified endpoint positions.

? The output device is then directed to fill in those positions between the end points with some color.

? For some device such as a pen plotter or random scan display, a straight line can be drawn smoothly from one end point to other.

? Digital devices display a straight line segment by plotting discrete points between the two endpoints.

? Discrete coordinate positions along the line path are calculated from the equation of the line.

? For a raster video display, the line intensity is loaded in frame buffer at the corresponding pixel positions.

? Reading from the frame buffer, the video controller then plots the screen pixels.

? Screen locations are referenced with integer values, so plotted positions may only approximate actual line positions between two specified endpoints.

? For example line position of (12.36, 23.87) would be converted to pixel position (12, 24).

? This rounding of coordinate values to integers causes lines to be displayed with a stair step appearance

("the jaggies"),

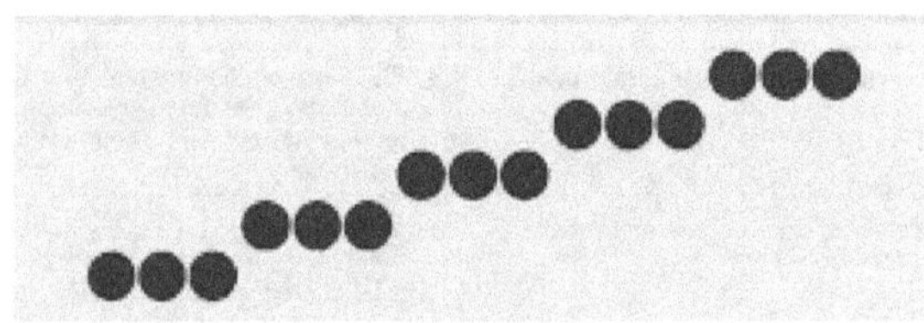

Stair step effect produced when line is generated as a series of pixel positions.

? The stair step shape is noticeable in low resolution system, and we can improve their appearance somewhat by displaying them on high resolution system.

? More effective techniques for smoothing raster lines are based on adjusting pixel intensities along the line paths.

? For raster graphics device-level algorithms discuss here, object positions are specified directly in integer device coordinates.

? Pixel position will referenced according to scan-line number and column number

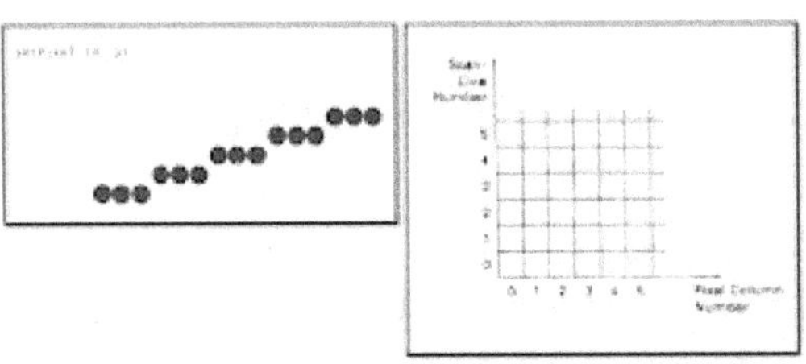

Pixel positions referenced by scan-
line number and column number.

? To load the specified color into the frame buffer at a particular position, we will assume we have available low-level procedure of the form ????????(?, ?).

? Similarly for retrieve the current frame buffer intensity we assume to have procedure ????????(?, ?).

Line Drawing Algorithms

? The Cartesian slop-intercept equation for a straight line is

? = ?? + ?

with '?' representing slop and '?' as the Y intercept.

? The two endpoints of the line are given which are say (?1, ?1) and (?2, ?2).

Line path between endpoint positions.

? We can determine values for the slope m by equation:

? = (?2 − ?1)/(?2 − ?1)

? We can determine values for the intercept b by equation:

? = ?1 − ? * ?1

? For the given interval Δ? along a line, we can compute the corresponding ? interval Δ? as:

Δ? = ? * Δ?

? Similarly for Δ?:

Δ? = Δ?/?

? For line with slop |?| < 1, Δ? can be set proportional to small horizontal deflection voltage and the corresponding vertical deflection voltage is then set proportional to Δ? which is calculated from above equation.

? For line with slop |?| > 1, Δ? can be set proportional to small vertical deflection voltage and the corresponding horizontal deflection voltage is then set proportional to Δ? which is calculated from above equation.

? For line with slop ? = 1, Δ? = Δ? and the horizontal and vertical deflection voltages are equal.

DDA Algorithm

? Digital differential analyzer (DDA) is scan conversion line drawing algorithm based on calculating either

Δ? or Δ? using above equation.

? We sample the line at unit intervals in one coordinate and find corresponding integer values nearest the line path for the other coordinate.

? Consider first a line with positive slope and slope is less than or equal to 1:

We sample at unit x interval (Δ? = 1) and calculate each successive y value as follow:

? = ? * ? + ?

?? = ? * (? + 1) + ?

In general ?? = ? * (? + ?) + ? , &

??+1 = ? * (? + ? + 1) + ?

  Now write this equation in form:

??+1 − ?? = (? * (? + ? + 1) + ?) − (? * (? + ?) + ?)

??+1 = ?? + ?

So that it is computed fast in computer as addition is fast compare to multiplication.

? In above equation ? takes integer values starting from 1 and increase by 1 until the final endpoint is reached.

? As ? can be any real number between 0 and 1, the calculated ? values must be rounded to the nearest integer.

? Consider a case for a line with a positive slope greater than 1:

We change the role of ? and ? that is sample at unit ? intervals (Δ? = 1) and calculate each succeeding

? value as:

? = (? − ?)/?

?1 = ((? + 1) − ?)/?

In general ?? = ((? + ?) − ?)/?, &

??+1 = ((? + ? + 1) − ?)/?

Now write this equation in form:

??+1 − ?? = (((? + ? + 1) − ?)/?) − (((? + ?) − ?)/?)

??+1 = ?? + 1/?

? Above both equations are based on the assumption that lines are to be processed from left endpoint to the right endpoint.

? If we processed line from right endpoint to left endpoint than: If Δ? = −1 equation become:

??+1 = ?? − ?

If Δ? = −1 equation become:

??+1 = ?? − 1/?

? Above calculated equations also used to calculate pixel position along a line with negative slope.

Procedure for DDA line algorithm.

```
Void lineDDA (int xa, int ya, int xb, int yb)
{
int dx = xb − xa, dy = yb − ya, steps, k;
float xincrement, yincrement, x = xa, y = ya; if (abs(dx)>abs(dy))
{
}
else
{
}
Steps = abs (dx);
Steps = abs (dy);
    xincrement = dx/(float) steps; yincrement = dy/(float) steps;
setpixel (ROUND (x), ROUND (y)); for(k=0;k<steps;k++)
{
x += xincrement; y += yincrement;
setpixel (ROUND (x), ROUND (y));
}
}
```

Advantages of DDA algorithm

? It is faster algorithm.

? It is simple algorithm.

Disadvantage of DDA algorithm

? Floating point arithmetic is time consuming.

? Poor end point accuracy.

Bresenham's Line Algorithm

? An accurate and efficient raster line-generating algorithm, developed by Bresenham which scan converts line using only incremental integer calculations that can be modified to display circles and other curves.

? Figure shows section of display screen where straight line segments are to be drawn.

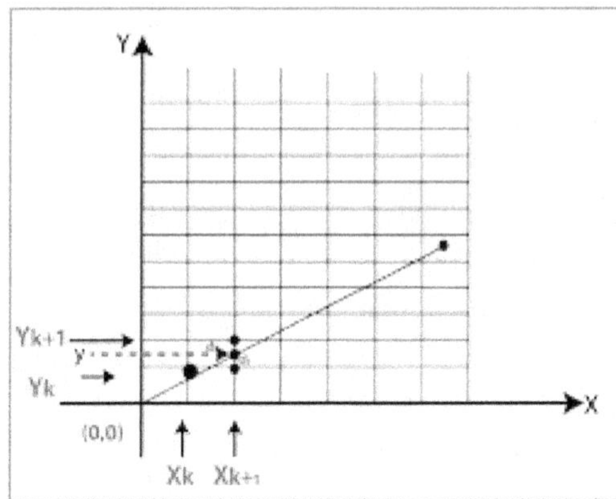

? The vertical axes show scan-line positions and the horizontal axes identify pixel column.

? Sampling at unit ? intervals in these examples, we need to decide which of two possible pixel position is closer to the line path at each sample step.

? To illustrate bresenham's approach, we first consider the scan-conversion process for lines with positive slope less than 1.

? Pixel positions along a line path are then determined by sampling at unit ? intervals.

? Starting from left endpoint $(?_0, ?_0)$ of a given line, we step to each successive column and plot the pixel whose scan-line ? value is closest to the line path.

? Assuming we have determined that the pixel at $(??, ??)$ is to be displayed, we next need to decide which pixel to plot in column $?? + 1$.

? Our choices are the pixels at positions $(?? + 1, ??)$ and $(?? + 1, ?? + 1)$.

? Let's see mathematical calculation used to decide which pixel position is light up.

? We know that equation of line is:

$? = ?? + ?$

Now for position $?? + 1$.

$? = ?(?? + 1) + ?$

? Now calculate distance bet actual line's ? value and lower pixel as $?1$ and distance bet actual line's ?

value and upper pixel as $?2$.

$?1 = ? - ??$

d1 = m(xk + 1) + b – yk

----

(1)

?2 = (?? + 1) – ?

?2 = (?? + 1) – ?(?? + 1) – ? ....(2)

? Now calculate ?1 – ?2 from equation (1) and (2).

?1 – ?2 = (? – ??) – ((?? + 1) – ?)

?1 – ?2 = {?(?? + 1) + ? – ??} – {(?? + 1) – ?(?? + 1) – ?}

?1 – ?2 = {??? + ? + ? – ??} – {?? + 1 – ??? – ? – ?}

?1 – ?2 = 2?(?? + 1) – 2?? + 2? – 1 ....(3)

? Now substitute ? = Δ?/Δ? in equation (3)

?1 – ?2 = 2 (Δ?) (?? + 1) – 2?? + 2? – 1 ....(4)

? Now we have decision parameter ?? for ??h step in the line algorithm is given by:

?? = Δ?(?1 – ?2)

?? = Δ?(2Δ?/Δ?(?? + 1) – 2?? + 2? – 1)

?? = 2Δ??? + 2Δ? – 2Δ??? + 2Δ?? – Δ?

?? = 2Δ??? – 2Δ??? + 2Δ? + 2Δ?? – Δ? ....(5)

?? = 2Δ??? – 2Δ??? + ? (?h??? ???????? ? = 2Δ? + 2Δ?? – Δ?) .... (6)

? The sign of ?? is the same as the sign of ?1 – ?2, since Δ? > 0 for our example.

? Parameter ? is constant which is independent of pixel position and will eliminate in the recursive calculation for ??.

? Now if ?? is negative then we plot the lower pixel otherwise we plot the upper pixel.

? So successive decision parameters using incremental integer calculation as:

??+1 = 2Δ???+1 – 2Δ???+1 + C

? Now Subtract ?? from ??+1

??+1 – ?? = 2Δ?(??+1 – ??) – 2Δ?(??+1 – ??)

??+1 – ?? = 2Δ???+1 – 2Δ???+1 + C – 2Δ??? + 2Δ??? – C

But ??+1 = ?? + 1, so that (??+1 – ??) = 1

??+1 = ?? + 2Δ? – 2Δ?(??+1 – ??)

? Where the terms ??+1 – ?? is either 0 or 1, depends on the sign of parameter ??.

? This recursive calculation of decision parameters is performed at each integer ? position starting at the left coordinate endpoint of the line.

? The first decision parameter ?0 is calculated using equation (5) as first time we need to take constant part into account so:

?? = 2Δ??? – 2Δ??? + 2Δ? + 2Δ?? – Δ?

?0 = 2Δ??0 – 2Δ??0 + 2Δ? + 2Δ?? – Δ?

Now ?????????? ? = ?0 – ??0

?0 = 2Δ??0 – 2Δ??0 + 2Δ? + 2Δ?(?0 – ??0) – Δx

Now Substitute ? = Δ?/??

?0 = 2Δ??0 – 2Δ??0 + 2Δ? + 2Δ?(?0 – (Δ?/Δ?)?0) – Δx

?0 = 2Δ??0 – 2Δ??0 + 2Δ? + 2Δ??0 – 2Δ??0 – Δx

?0 = 2Δ? – Δx

Parallel Execution of Line Algorithms

? The line-generating algorithms we have discussed so far determine pixel positions sequentially.

? With parallel computer we can calculate pixel position along a line path simultaneously by dividing work among the various processors available.

? One way to use multiple processors is partitioning existing sequential algorithm into small parts and compute separately.

? Alternatively we can go for other ways to setup the processing so that pixel positions can be calculated efficiently in parallel.

? Important point to be taking into account while devising parallel algorithm is to balance the load among the available processors.

? Given ?? number of processors we can set up parallel Bresenham line algorithm by subdividing the line path into ?? partitions and simultaneously generating line segment in each of the subintervals.

? For a line with slope 0 < ? < 1 and left endpoint coordinate position (?0, ?0), we partition the line along the positive ? direction.

? The distance between beginning ? positions of adjacent partitions can be calculated as:

Δ?? = (Δ? + ?? – 1)/??

Were Δ? is the width of the line. And value for partition with Δ?? is computed using integer division.

? Numbering the partitions and the processors, as 0, 1, 2, up to ?? – ?, we calculate the starting ?

coordinate for the ??h partition as:

?? = ?0 + ?Δ??

? To apply Bresenham's algorithm over the partitions, we need the initial value for the ? coordinate and the initial value for the decision parameter in each partition.

? The change Δ?? in the ? direction over each partition is calculated from the line slope m and partition width Δ??:

Δ?? = ?Δ??

? At the ??h partition, the starting ? coordinate is then

?? = ?0 + ?????(?Δ??)

? The initial decision parameter for Bresenham's algorithm at the start of the ??h subinterval is obtained from Equation(6):

?? = 2Δ??? − 2Δ??? + 2Δ? + 2Δ?? − Δ?

? = 2Δ?(? + ?Δ?) − 2Δ?(? + ?????(?Δ?)) + 2Δ? + 2Δ?(?

− Δ? ?

) − Δ?

? 0 ? 0 ?

0 Δ? 0

e

?? = 2Δ??0 − 2Δ??Δ?? − 2Δ??0 − 2Δ??????(?Δ??) + 2Δ? + 2Δ??0 − 2Δ??0 − Δ?

?? = 2Δ??Δ?? − 2Δ??????(?Δ??) + 2Δ? − Δ?

? Each processor then calculates pixel positions over its assigned subinterval.

? The extension of the parallel Bresenham algorithm to a line with slope greater than 1 is achieved by partitioning the line in the ? direction and calculating beginning ? values for the positions.

? For negative slopes, we increment coordinate values in one direction and decrement in the other.

Bounding box for a line with coordinate extents Δx and Δy.

? Another way to set up parallel algorithms on raster system is to assign each processor to a particular group of screen pixels.

? With sufficient number of processor we can assign each processor to one pixel within some screen region.

? This approach can be adapted to line display by assigning one processor to each of the pixels within the limit of the bounding rectangle and calculating pixel distance from the line path.

? The number of pixels within the bounding rectangle of a line is $\Delta? \times \Delta?$.

? Perpendicular distance ? from line to a particular pixel is calculated by:

$? = ?? + ?? + ?$

Where

$? = -\Delta?/????????h$

$? = -\Delta?/????????h$

$? = (?0\Delta? - ?0\Delta?)/????????h$

With

$????????h = \sqrt{\Delta?2 + \Delta?2}$

? Once the constant ?, ?, and ? have been evaluated for the line each processors need to perform two multiplications and two additions to compute the pixel distance ?.

? A pixel is plotted if d is less than a specified line thickness parameter.

? Instead of partitioning the screen into single pixels, we can assign to each processor either a scan line or a column a column of pixels depending on the line slope.

Each processor then calculates pixel positions over its assigned subinterval.

? The extension of the parallel Bresenham algorithm to a line with slope greater than 1 is achieved by partitioning the line in the ? direction and calculating beginning ? values for the positions.

? For negative slopes, we increment coordinate values in one direction and decrement in the other.

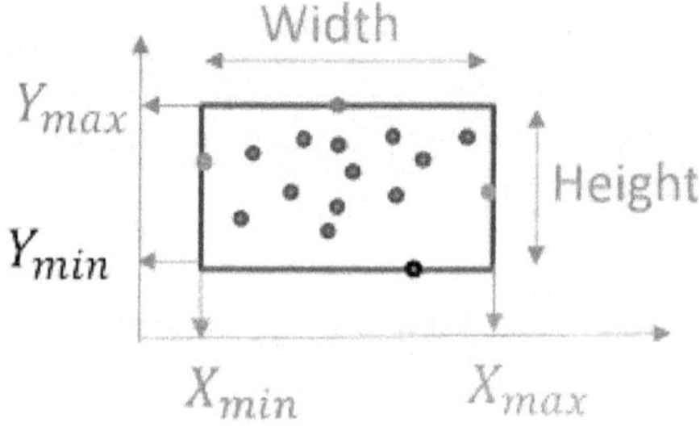

? Another way to set up parallel algorithms on raster system is to assign each processor to a particular group of screen pixels.

? With sufficient number of processor we can assign each processor to one pixel within some screen region.

? This approach can be adapted to line display by assigning one processor to each of the pixels within the limit of the bounding rectangle and calculating pixel distance from the line path.

? The number of pixels within the bounding rectangle of a line is $\Delta? \times \Delta?$.

? Perpendicular distance ? from line to a particular pixel is calculated by:

$? = ?? + ?? + ?$

Where

$? = -\Delta? / ????????? h$

$? = -\Delta? / ????????? h$

$? = (?0\Delta? - ?0\Delta?) / ????????? h$

With

$????????? h = \sqrt{\Delta?2 + \Delta?2}$

? Once the constant ?, ?, and ? have been evaluated for the line each processors need to perform two multiplications and two additions to compute the pixel distance ?.

? A pixel is plotted if d is less than a specified line thickness parameter.

? Instead of partitioning the screen into single pixels, we can assign to each processor either a scan line or a column a column of pixels depending on the line slope.

Each processor calculates line intersection with horizontal row or vertical column of pixels assigned to that processor.

? If vertical column is assign to processor then ? is fix and it will calculate ? and similarly is horizontal row is assign to processor then ? is fix and ? will be calculated.

? Such direct methods are slow in sequential machine but we can perform very efficiently using multiple processors.

Circle

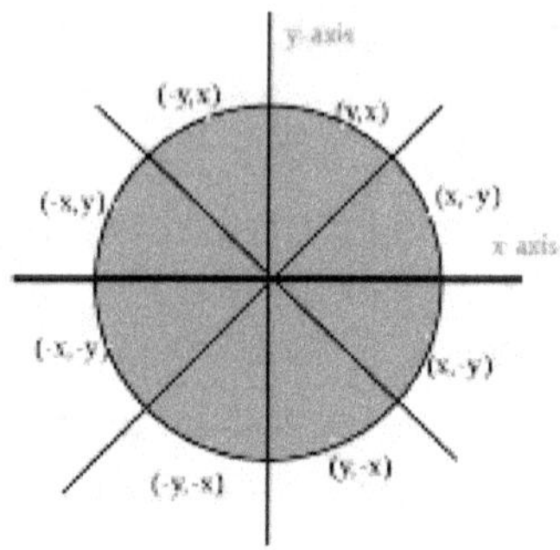

For a pixel (x,y) all possible pixels in 8 octants.

Circle with center coordinates (??, ??) and radius ?.

? A circle is defined as the set of points that are all at a given distance r from a center position say (??, ??).

Properties of Circle

? The distance relationship is expressed by the Pythagorean theorem in Cartesian coordinates as:

$(? – ??)2 + (? – ??)2 = ?2$

? We could use this equation to calculate circular boundary points by incrementing 1 in ? direction in every steps from ?? – ? to ?? + ? and calculate corresponding ? values at each position as:

$(? – ??)2 + (? – ??)2 = ?2$

$(? – ??)2 = ?2 – (? – ??)2$

$(? – ??) = ±√?2 – (?? – ?)2$

$y = ?? ± √?2 – (?? – ?)2$

? But this is not best method for generating a circle because it requires more number of calculations which take more time to execute.

? And also spacing between the plotted pixel positions is not uniform

We can adjust spacing by stepping through ? values and calculating ? values whenever the absolute value of the slop of the circle is greater than 1. But it will increases computation processing requirement.

? Another way to eliminate the non-uniform spacing is to draw circle using polar coordinates '?' and ''.

? Calculating circle boundary using polar equation is given by pair of equations which is as follows.

$? = ?? + ? cos$

? = ?? + ? sin

? When display is produce using these equations using fixed angular step size circle is plotted with uniform spacing.

? The step size ' ' is chosen according to application and display device.

? For a more continuous boundary on a raster display we can set the step size at 1/?. This plot pixel position that are approximately one unit apart.

? Computation can be reduced by considering symmetry city property of circles. The shape of circle is similar in each quadrant.

? We can obtain pixel position in second quadrant from first quadrant using reflection about ? axis and similarly for third and fourth quadrant from second and first respectively using reflection about ? axis.

? We can take one step further and note that there is also symmetry between octants. Circle sections in adjacent octant within one quadrant are symmetric with respect to the 450 line dividing the two octants.

? This symmetry condition is shown in figure below where point (?, ?) on one circle sector is mapped in other seven sector of circle.

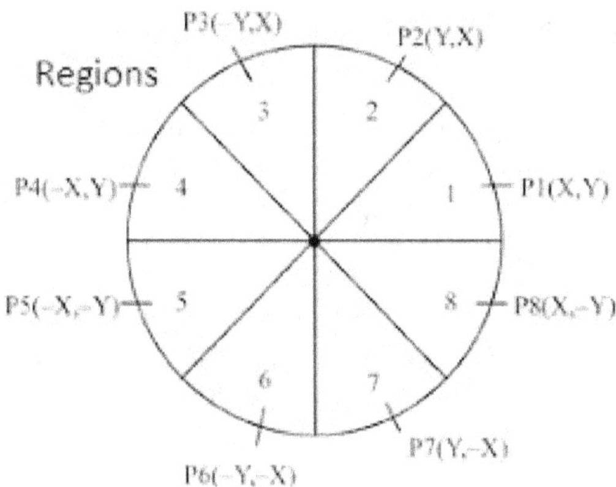

symmetry of circle

Taking advantage of this symmetry property of circle we can generate all pixel position on boundary of circle by calculating only one sector from ? = 0 to ? = ?.

? Determining pixel position along circumference of circle using any of two equations shown above still required large computation.

? More efficient circle algorithm are based on incremental calculation of decision parameters, as in the Bresenham line algorithm.

? Bresenham's line algorithm can be adapted to circle generation by setting decision parameter for finding

closest pixel to the circumference at each sampling step.

? The Cartesian coordinate circle equation is nonlinear so that square root evaluations would be required to compute pixel distance from circular path.

? Bresenham's circle algorithm avoids these square root calculation by comparing the square of the pixel separation distance.

? A method for direct distance comparison to test the midpoint between two pixels to determine if this midpoint is inside or outside the circle boundary.

? This method is easily applied to other conics also.

? Midpoint approach generates same pixel position as generated by bresenham's circle algorithm.

? The error involve in locating pixel positions along any conic section using midpoint test is limited to one- half the pixel separation.

Midpoint Circle Algorithm

? Similar to raster line algorithm we sample at unit interval and determine the closest pixel position to the specified circle path at each step.

? Given radius '?' and center (??, ??)

? We first setup our algorithm to calculate circular path coordinates for center (0, 0). And then we will transfer calculated pixel position to center (??, ??) by adding ?? to ? and ?? to ?.

? Along the circle section from ? = 0 to ? = ? in the first quadrant, the slope of the curve varies from 0 to -1 so we can step unit step in positive ? direction over this octant and use a decision parameter to determine which of the two possible ? position is closer to the circular path.

? Position in the other seven octants are then obtain by symmetry.

? For the decision parameter we use the circle function which is:

???????(?, ?) = ?2 + ?2 − ?2

? Any point which is on the boundary is satisfied ???????(?, ?) = 0 if the point is inside circle function value is negative and if point is outside circle the function value is positive which can be summarize as below.

< 0 ?? (?, ?)?? ?????? ?*h*? ?????? ????????

???????(?, ?) = 0 ?? (?, ?)?? ?? ?*h*? ?????? ????????

> 0 ?? (?, ?)?? ??????? ?*h*? ?????? ????????

? Above equation we calculate for the mid positions between pixels near the circular path at each sampling step and we setup incremental calculation for this function as we did in the line algorithm.

? Below figure shows the midpoint between the two candidate pixels at sampling position $?? + 1$.

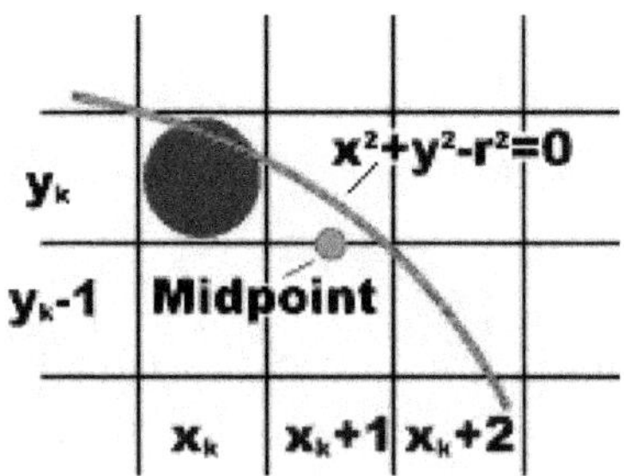

Midpoint between candidate pixel at sampling position $?? + 1$ along circle path.

? Assuming we have just plotted the pixel at $(??, ??)$ and next we need to determine whether the pixel at
position '$(?? + 1, ??)$' or the one at position' $(?? + 1, ?? - 1)$' is closer to circle boundary.

? So for finding which pixel is more closer using decision parameter evaluated at the midpoint between two candidate pixels as below:

$?? = ??????? (?? + 1, ?? - 1)$

$= (??+1)2+(??-12)2-?2$

? If $?? < 0$ this midpoint is inside the circle and the pixel on the scan line $??$ is closer to circle boundary. Otherwise the midpoint is outside or on the boundary and we select the scan line $?? - 1$.

? Successive decision parameters are obtain using incremental calculations as follows:

$??+1 = ??????? (??+1 + 1, ??+1 - 1)$

$=[(??+1)+1]2+(??+1-12)2-?2$

(Or)

$??+1 = ?? + 2(?? + 1) + (??+12 - ??2) - (??+1 - ??) + 1$

? The initial decision parameter is obtained by evaluating the circle function at the start position
$(?0, ?0) = (0, ?)$ as follows.

$?0 =??????? (0 + 1, ? - 12)$

=1+(?−1 2)2− ?2

Or

?0= 5 4 -r

Algorithm for Midpoint Circle Generation

1. Input radius ? and circle center (??, ??), and obtain the first point on the circumference of a circle centered on the origin as

(?0, ?0) = (0, ?)

2. calculate the initial value of the decision parameter as

? = 5 − ?

4

3. At each ?? position, starting at ? = 0, perform the following test:

If ?? < 0, the next point along the circle centered on (0, 0) is (?? + 1, ??) &

??+1 = ?? + 2??+1 + 1

Otherwise, the next point along the circle is (?? + 1, ?? − 1) &

??+1 = ?? + 2??+1 + 1 − 2??+1

Where 2??+1 = 2?? + 2, & 2??+1 = 2?? − 2.

4. Determine symmetry points in the other seven octants.

5. Move each calculated pixel position (?, ?) onto the circular path centered on (??, ??) and plot the coordinate values:

? = ? + ??, ? = ? + ??

6. Repeat steps 3 through 5 until ? ≥ ?.

Ellipse

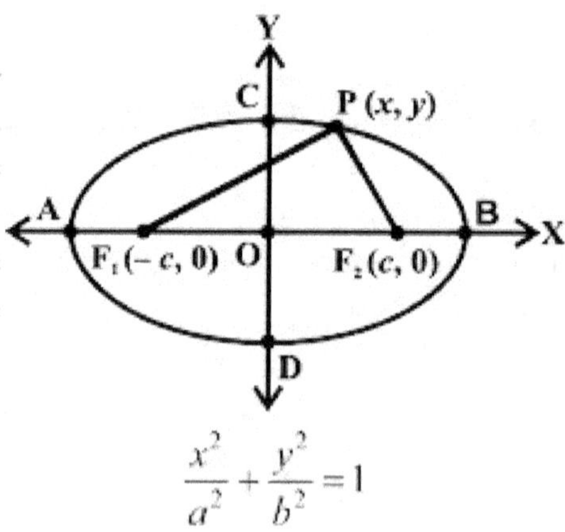

$$\frac{x^2}{a^2} + \frac{y^2}{b^2} = 1$$

Ellipse generated about foci f1 and f2.

? AN ellipse is defined as the set of points such that the sum of the distances from two fixed positions (foci) is same for all points.

Properties of Ellipse

? If we labeled distance from two foci to any point on ellipse boundary as ?1 and ?2 then the general equation of an ellipse can be written as follow.

?1 + ?2 = ????????

? Expressing distance in terms of focal coordinates ?1 = (?1, ?1) and ?2 = (?2, ?2) we have

√(? − ?1)2 + (? − ?1)2 + √(? − ?2)2 + (? − ?2)2 = ????????

? An interactive method for specifying an ellipse in an arbitrary orientation is to input two foci and a point on the ellipse boundary.

? With this three coordinates we can evaluate constant in equation:

√(? − ?1)2 + (? − ?1)2 + √(? − ?2)2 + (? − ?2)2 = ??????d

? We can also write this equation in the form

??2 + ??2 + ??? + ?? + ?? + ? = 0

? Where the coefficients ?, ?, ?, ?, ?, and ? are evaluated in terms of the focal coordinates and the dimensions of the major and minor axes of the ellipse.

? Major axis of an ellipse is straight line segment passing through both foci and extends up to boundary on both sides.

? The minor axis spans shortest dimension of ellipse, it bisect the major axis at right angle in two equal half.

? Then coefficient in ??2 + ??2 + ??? + ?? + ?? + ? = 0 can be evaluated and used to generate pixels along the elliptical path.

? Ellipse equation are greatly simplified if we align major and minor axis with coordinate axes i.e. ? − ????

and ? − ????.

? We can say ellipse is in standard position if their major and minor axes are parallel to ? − ???? and ? −

???? which is shown in below figure.

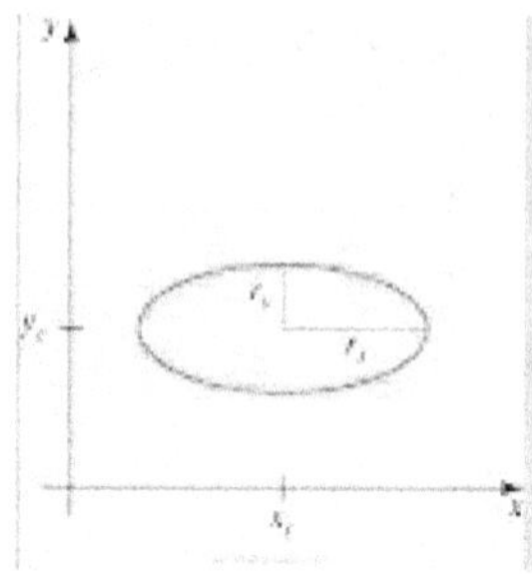

Ellipse centered at (??, ??) with semi major axis ?? and semi minor axis ?? are parallel to coordinate axis.

Equation of ellipse shown in figure 2.12 can be written in terms of the ellipse center coordinates and

parameters ?? and ?? as.

? – ?? 2 ? – ?? 2

(??) + (??) = 1

? Using the polar coordinates ? and ?, we can also describe the ellipse in standard position with the parametric equations:

? = ?? + ?? cos θ

? = ?? + ?? sin θ

? Symmetry considerations can be used to further reduced computations.

? An ellipse in standard position is symmetric between quadrants but unlike a circle it is not symmetric between octant.

? Thus we must calculate boundary point for one quadrant and then other three quadrants point can be obtained by symmetry as shown in figure below.

Midpoint Ellipse Algorithm

? Midpoint ellipse algorithm is a method for drawing ellipses in computer graphics. This method is modified from Bresenham's algorithm.

? The advantage of this modified method is that only addition operations are required in the program loops.

? This leads to simple and fast implementation in all processors.

? Given parameters ??, ?? and (??, ??) we determine points (?, ?) for an ellipse in standard position centered on the origin, and then we shift the points so the ellipse is centered at (??, ??).

? If we want to display the ellipse in nonstandard position then we rotate the ellipse about its center to
align with required direction.

? For the present we consider only the standard position.

? In this method we divide first quadrant into two parts according to the slope of an ellipse as shown in figure below.

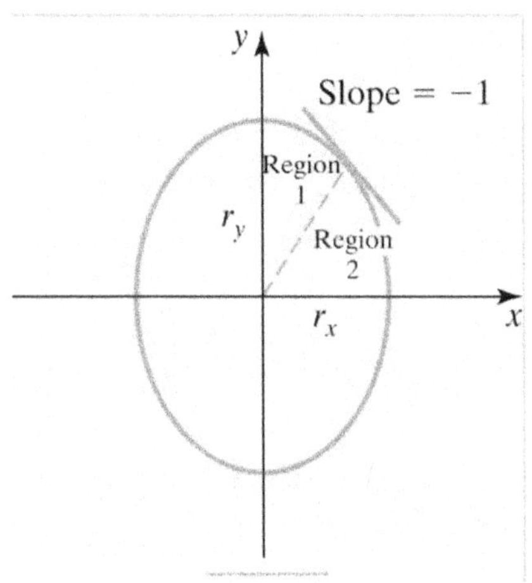

Ellipse processing regions. Over the region 1 the magnitude of ellipse slope is < 1 and over the region 2 the magnitude of ellipse slope > 1.

? We take unit step in ? direction if magnitude of slope is less than 1 in that region otherwise we take unit step in ? direction.

? Boundary divides region at ????? = −1.

? With ?? < ?? we process this quadrant by taking unit steps in ? direction in region 1 and unit steps in ?
direction in region 2.

? Region 1 and 2 can be processed in various ways.

? We can start from (0, ??) and step clockwise along the elliptical path in the first quadrant shifting from unit step in ? to unit step in ? when slope becomes less than -1.

? Alternatively, we could start at (??, 0) and select points in a counterclockwise order, shifting from unit steps in ? to unit steps in ? when the slope becomes greater than -1.

? With parallel processors, we could calculate pixel positions in the two regions simultaneously.

? Here we consider sequential implementation of midpoint algorithm. We take the start position at (0, ??)
and steps along the elliptical path in clockwise order through the first quadrant.

? We define ellipse function for center of ellipse at (0, 0) as follows.

(,)=2222−22

Which has the following properties:

< 0 ?? (?, ?)?? ?????? ?h? ??????? ????????

???????(?, ?) = 0 ?? (?, ?)?? ?? ?h? ??????? ????????

> 0 ?? (?, ?)?? ??????? ?h? ??????? ????????

? Thus the ellipse function serves as the decision parameter in the midpoint ellipse algorithm.

? At each sampling position we select the next pixel from two candidate pixel.

? Starting at (0, ??) we take unit step in ? direction until we reach the boundary between region 1 and 2 then we switch to unit steps in ? direction in remaining portion on ellipse in first quadrant.

? At each step we need to test the value of the slope of the curve for deciding the end point of the region-
1.

? The ellipse slope is calculated using following equation. 2222

? At boundary between region 1 and 2 ????? = −1 and equation become.
2??2? = 2??2?

? Therefore we move out of region 1 whenever following equation is false
2??2? ≤ 2??2?

? Following figure shows the midpoint between the two candidate pixels at sampling position ?? + 1 in the first region.

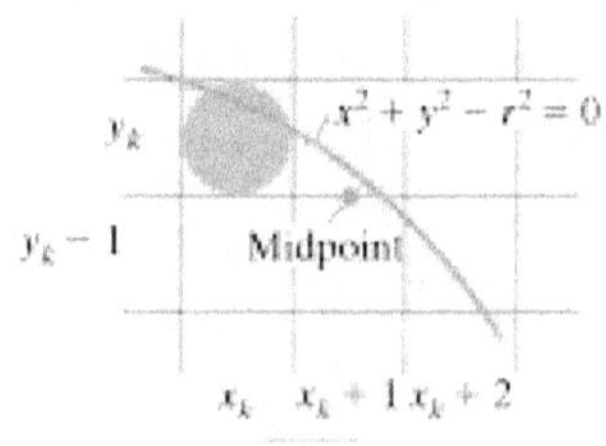

Midpoint between candidate pixels at sampling position $?? + 1$ along an elliptical path.

- Assume we are at (x_k, y_k) position and we determine the next position along the ellipse path by evaluating decision parameter at midpoint between two candidate pixels.

$$p_k^1 = f_{ellipse}\left(x_k + 1, y_k - \frac{1}{2}\right)$$
$$= r_y^2(x_k + 1)^2 + r_x^2\left(y_k - \frac{1}{2}\right)^2 - r_x^2 r_y^2$$

- If $p1_k < 0$, the midpoint is inside the ellipse and the pixel on scan line y_k is closer to ellipse boundary otherwise the midpoint is outside or on the ellipse boundary and we select the pixel $y_k - 1$.
- At the next sampling position decision parameter for region 1 is evaluated as.

$$p_{k+1}^1 = f_{ellipse}\left(x_{k+1} + 1, y_{k+1} - \frac{1}{2}\right)$$
$$= r_y^2[(x_k + 1) + 1]^2 + r_x^2\left(y_{k+1} - \frac{1}{2}\right)^2 - r_x^2 r_y^2 \mid$$

Line Attributes

? Basic attributes of a straight line segment are

1. Line Type
2. Line width
3. Line color
4. Pen and Brush option

    1. Line Type

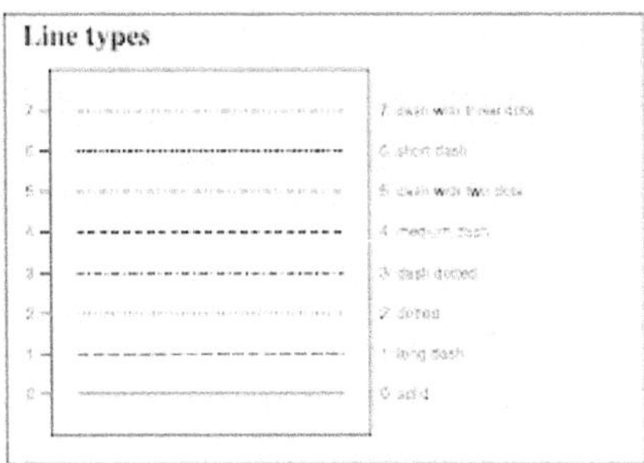

? Possible selection for the line-type attribute includes solid lines, dashed lines, and dotted lines etc.

? we modify a line –drawing algorithm to generate such lines by setting the length and spacing of displayed solid sections along the line path.

? A dashed line could be displayed by generating an inter dash spacing that is equal to the length of the solid sections. Both the length of the dashes and the inter dash spacing are often specified as user options.

? To set line type attributes in a PHIGS application program, a user invokes the function:

setLinetype(It)

? Where parameter lt is assigned a positive integer value of 1, 2, 3, 4... etc. to generate lines that are, respectively solid, dashed, dotted, or dash-dotted etc.

? Other values for the line-type parameter It could be used to display variations in the dot-dash patterns. Once the line-type parameter has been set in a PHIGS application program, all subsequent line-drawing commands produce lines with this Line type.

? Raster graphics generates these types by plottingsome pixel and some pixel is off along the line path. We can generate different patterns by specifying 1 for on pixel and 0 for off pixel then we can generate 1010101 patter as a dotted line.

? It is used in many application for example comparing data in graphical form.

Line Width

? Implementation of line-width options depends on the capabilities of the output device.

? A heavy line on a video monitor could be displayed as adjacent parallel lines, while a pen plotter might require pen changes.

? To set line width attributes in a PHIGS application program, a user invokes the function:

setLinewidthScalFactor (lw)

? Line-width parameter lw is assigned a positive number to indicate the relative width of the line to be displayed.

? Values greater than 1 produce lines thicker than the standard line width and values less than the 1 produce line thinner than the standard line width.

? In raster graphics we generate thick line by plotting above and below pixel of line path when slope

|?| < 1 and by plotting left and right pixel of line path when slope |?| > 1

which is illustrated in below figure.

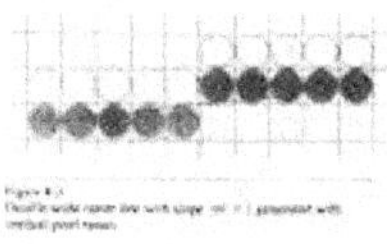

Pen and Brush Options

? In some graphics packages line is displayed with pen and brush selections.

? Options in this category include shape, size, and pattern.

? Some possible pen or brush are shown in below figure.

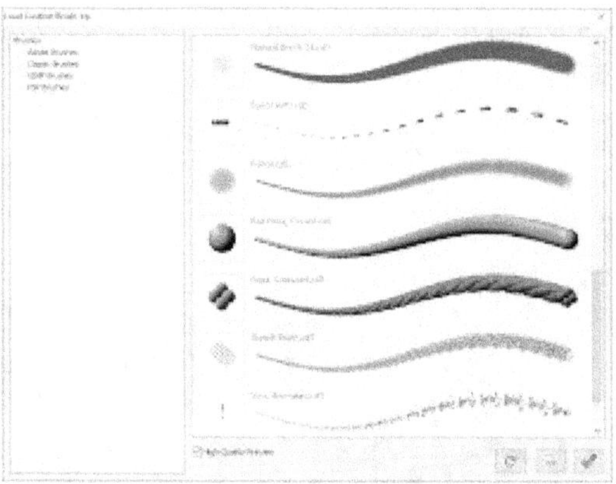

? These shapes can be stored in a pixel mask that identifies the array of pixel positions that are to be set along the line path.

? Lines generated with pen (or brush) shapes can be displayed in various widths by changing the size of the mask.

? Also, lines can be displayed with selected patterns by superimposing the pattern values onto the pen or brush mask.

Color and Grayscale Levels

? Various color and intensity-level options can be made available to a user, depending on the capabilities and design objectives of a particular system.

? General purpose raster-scan systems, for example, usually provide a wide range of colors, while random- scan monitors typically offer only a few color choices, if any.

? In a color raster system, the number of color choices available depends on the amount of storage provided per pixel in the frame buffer

? Also, color-information can be stored in the frame buffer in two ways: We can store color codes directly in the frame buffer, or we can put the color codes in a separate table and use pixel values as an index into this table

? With direct storage scheme we required large memory for frame buffer when we display more color.

? While in case of table it is reduced and we call it color table or color lookup table.

Color Lookup Table

? Color values of 24 bit is stored in lookup table and in frame buffer we store only 8 bit index which gives index of required color stored into lookup table. So that size of frame buffer is reduced and we can display more color.

? When we display picture using this technique on output screen we look into frame buffer where index of the color is stored and take 24 bit color value from look up table corresponding to frame buffer index value and display that color on particular pixel.

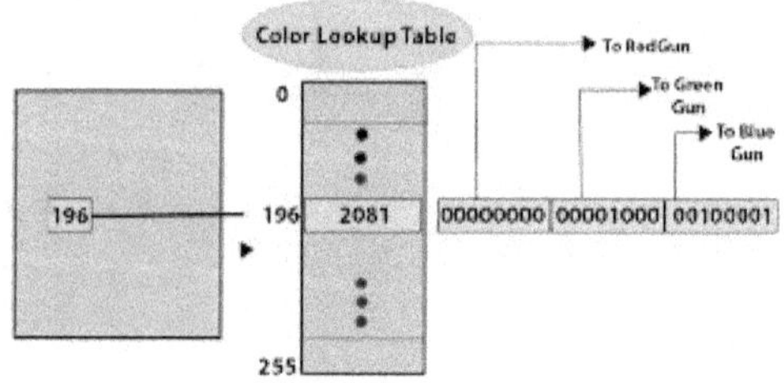

Grayscale

? With monitors that have no color capability, color function can be used in an application program to set the shades of grey, or greyscale for display primitives.

? Numeric values between 0-to-1 can be used to specify greyscale levels.

? This numeric values is converted in binary code for store in raster system.
? Table below shows specification for intensity codes for a four level greyscale system.

Intensity codes	Stored intensity values in frame Buffer		Displayed Grayscale
0.0	0	00	Black
0.33	1	01	Dark Gray
0.67	2	10	Light Gray
1.0	3	11	White

? In this example, any intensity input value near 0.33 would be stored as the binary value 01 in the frame buffer, and pixels with this value would be displayed as dark grey.
? If more bits are available per pixel we can obtain more levels of grey scale for example with 3 bit per pixel we can achieve 8 levels of greyscale.

Area-Fill Attributes

? For filling any area we have choice between solid colors or pattern to fill all these are include in area fill attributes.
? Area can be painted by various burses and style.

Fill Styles

? Area are generally displayed with three basic style hollow with color border, filled with solid color, or filled with some design.
? In PHIGS package fill style is selected by following function.
setInteriorStyle (fs)
? Value of fs include hollow, solid, pattern etc.
? Another values for fill style is hatch, which is patterns of line like parallel line or crossed line.
? Figure bellow shows different style of filling area.

- Figure bellow shows different style of filling area.

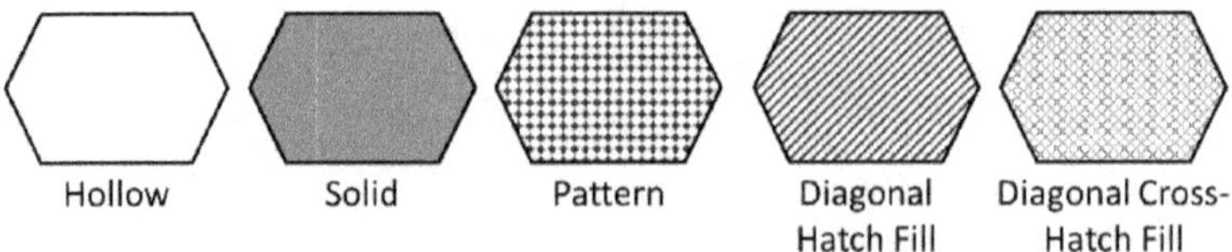

Fig. 2.36: - Different style of area filling.

- For setting interior color in PHIGS package we use:

setInteriorColorIndex (fc)

- Where fc specify the fill color.

Pattern Fill

? We select the pattern with

setInteriorStyleIndex (pi)

? Where pattern index parameter pi specifies position in pattern table entry.

? For example, the following set of statements would fill the area defined in the fillArea command with the second pattern type stored in the pattern table:

SetInteriorStyle(pattern) ; setInteriorStyleIndex (2) ; fillArea (n, points);

? Separate table can be maintain for hatch pattern and we can generate our own table with required pattern.

? Other function used for setting other style as follows

setpatternsize (dx, dy) setPaternReferencePoint (positicn)

? We can create our own pattern by setting and resetting group of pixel and then map it into the color matrix.

Soft Fill

? Soft fill is modified boundary fill and flood fill algorithm in which we are fill layer of color on back ground color so that we can obtain the combination of both color.

? It is used to recolor or repaint so that we can obtain layer of multiple color and get new color combination.

? One use of this algorithm is soften the fill at boundary so that blurred effect will reduce the aliasing effect.

? For example if we fill t amount of foreground color then pixel color is obtain as:

? $= ??$ $+ (1 - ?)?$

? Where F is foreground color and B is background color.

? If we use more than two color say three at that time equation becomes as follow:

? = ?0? + ?1?1 + (1 – ?0 – ?1)?2

? Where the sum of coefficient ?0, ?1, and (1 – ?0 – ?1) is 1.

Character Attributes

? The appearance of displayed characters is controlled by attributes such as font, size, color, and orientation.

? Attributes can be set for entire string or may be individually. Two types of character attribute.

1. Text attributes

2. Marker attributes

Text Attributes

? In text we are having so many style and design like italic fonts, bold fonts etc.

? For setting the font style in PHIGS package we have one function which is:
setTextFont (tf)

? Where tf is used to specify text font

? It will set specified font as a current character.

? For setting color of character in PHIGS we have function:
setTextColorIndex (tc)

? Where text color parameter tc specifies an allowable color code.

? For setting the size of the text we use function.
setCharacterheight (ch)

? For scaling the character we use function.
setCharacterExpansionFacter (cw)

? Where character width parameter cw is set to a positive real number that scale the character body width.

? Spacing between character is controlled by function
setCharacterSpacing (cs)

? Where character spacing parameter cs can be assigned any real value.

? The orientation for a displayed character string is set according to the direction of the character up vector:
setCharacterUpVector (upvect)

? Parameter upvect in this function is assigned two values that specify the ? and ? vector components.

? Text is then displayed so that the orientation of characters from baseline to cap line is in the direction of the up vector.

? For setting the path of the character we use function:

setTextPath (tp)

? Where the text path parameter tp can be assigned the value: right, left, up, or down.

? It will set the direction in which we are writing.

? For setting the alignment of the text we use function.

setTextAlignment (h, v)

? Where parameter h and v control horizontal and vertical alignment respectively.

? For specifying precision for text display is given with function.

setTextPrecision (tpr)

? Where text precision parameter tpr is assigned one of the values: string, char, or stroke.

? The highest-quality text is produced when the parameter is set to the value stroke.

Marker Attributes

? A marker symbol display single character in different color and in different sizes.

? For marker attributes implementation by procedure that load the chosen character into the raster at defined position with the specified color and size.

? We select marker type using function.

setMarkerType (mt)

? Where marker type parameter mt is set to an integer code.

? Typical codes for marker type are the integers 1 through 5, specifying, respectively, a dot (.), a vertical cross (+), an asterisk (*), a circle (o), and a diagonal cross (x). Displayed marker types are centred on the marker coordinates.

? We set the marker size with function.

SetMarkerSizeScaleFactor (ms)

? Where parameter marker size ms assigned a positive number according to need for scaling.

? For setting marker color we use function.

setPolymarkerColorIndex (mc)

? Where parameter mc specify the color of the marker symbol.

CHAPTER TWO

2D Geometric Transformations

Transformation

Changing Position, shape, size, or orientation of an object on display is known as transformation.

Basic Transformation

? Basic transformation includes three transformations Translation, Rotation, and Scaling.

? These three transformations are known as basic transformation because with combination of these three transformations we can obtain any transformation.

Translation

In Computer graphics, 2D Translation is a process of moving an object from one position to another in a two dimensional plane. Consider a point object O has to be moved from one position to another in a 2D plane. Tx defines the distance the Xold coordinate has to be moved.

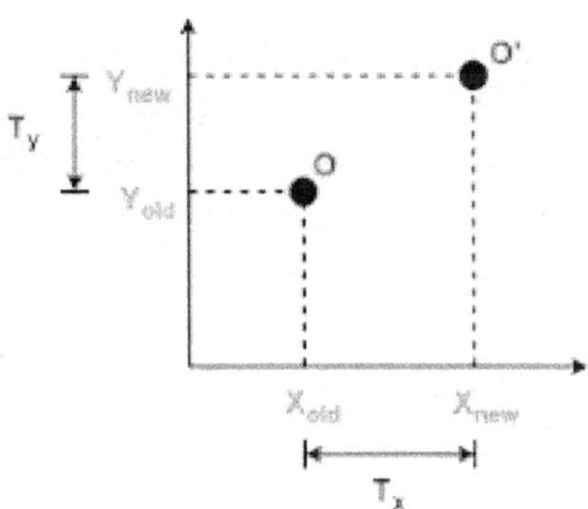

2D Translation in Computer Graphics

? It is a transformation that used to reposition the object along the straight line path from one coordinate location to another.

? It is rigid body transformation so we need to translate whole object.

? We translate two dimensional point by adding translation distance ?? and ?? to the original coordinate position (?, ?) to move at new position (?′, ?′) as:

?′ = ? + ?? & ?′ = ? + ??

? Translation distance pair (??,??) is called a Translation Vector or Shift Vector.

? We can represent it into single matrix equation in column vector as;

?′ = ? + ?

?′

[?′] =

? [?] +

?? [??]

? We can also represent it in row vector form as:

?′ = ? + ?

[?′ ?′] = [? ?] + [?? ??]

? Since column vector representation is standard mathematical notation and since many graphics package like GKS and PHIGS uses column vector we will also follow column vector representation.

Rotation

? It is a transformation that used to reposition the object along the circular path in the XY - plane.

? To generate a rotation we specify a rotation angle ? and the position of the Rotation Point (Pivot Point) (??,??) about which the object is to be rotated.

? Positive value of rotation angle defines counter clockwise rotation and negative value of rotation angle defines clockwise rotation.

? We first find the equation of rotation when pivot point is at coordinate origin(?, ?).

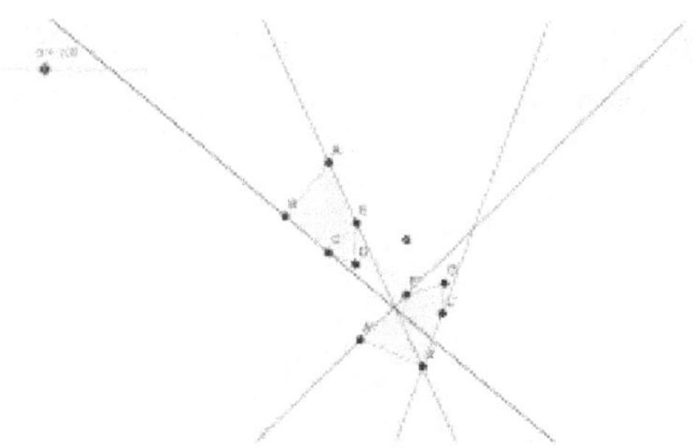

? From figure we can write.

? = ? ??? ∅

? = ? ??? ∅

and

?′ = ? ???(? + ∅) = ? ??? ∅ ??? ? − ? ??? ∅ ??? ?

?′ = ? ???(∅ + ?) = ? ??? ∅ ??? ? + ? ??? ∅ ??? ?

? Now replace ? ??? ∅ with ? and ? ??? ∅ with ? in above equation.

?′ = ? ??? ? − ? ??? ?

?′ = ? ??? ? + ? ??? ?

? Rotation about arbitrary point is illustrated in below figure.

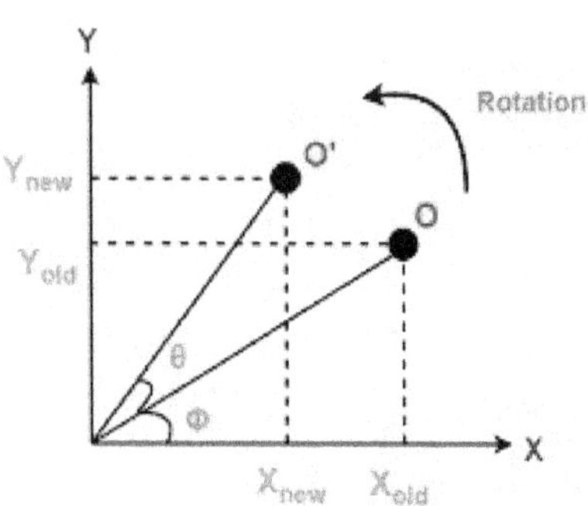

2D Rotation in Computer Graphics

? Transformation equation for rotation of a point about pivot point (??,??) is:

?′ = ?? + (? − ??) ??? ? − (? − ??) ??? ?

?′ = ?? + (? − ??) ??? ? + (? − ??) ??? ?

? These equations are differing from rotation about origin and its matrix representation is also different.

? Its matrix equation can be obtained by simple method that we will discuss later in this chapter.

? Rotation is also rigid body transformation so we need to rotate each point of object.

<u>Scaling</u>

? It is a transformation that used to alter the size of an object.

? This operation is carried out by multiplying coordinate value (?, ?) with scaling factor (??, ??)

respectively.

? So equation for scaling is given by:

?′ = ? · ??

?′ = ? · ??

These equation can be represented in column vector matrix equation as:

?′ = ? · ?

Any positive value can be assigned to (??, ??). Values less than 1 reduce the size while values

greater than 1 enlarge the size of object, and object remains unchanged when values

of both factor is 1.

? Same values of ?? and ?? will produce Uniform Scaling. And different values of ?? and ?? will produce

Differential Scaling.

? Objects transformed with above equation are both scale and repositioned.

? Scaling factor with value less than 1 will move object closer to origin, while scaling factor with value greater than 1 will move object away from origin.

? We can control the position of object after scaling by keeping one position fixed called Fix point (??, ??)

that point will remain unchanged after the scaling transformation.

? Equation for scaling with fixed point position as (??, ??) is:

?′ = ?? + (? − ??)?? ?′ = ?? + (? − ??)??

?′ = ?? + ??? − ???? ?′ = ?? + ??? − ????

?′ = ??? + ??(? − ??) ?′ = ??? + ??(? − ??)

? Matrix equation for the same will discuss in later section.

? Polygons are scaled by applying scaling at coordinates and redrawing while other body like circle and ellipse will scale using its defining parameters. For example ellipse will scale using its semi major axis, semi minor axis and center point scaling and redrawing at that position.

Matrix Representation and homogeneous coordinates

? Many graphics application involves sequence of geometric transformations.

? For example in design and picture construction application we perform Translation, Rotation, and scaling to fit the picture components into their proper positions.

? For efficient processing we will reformulate transformation sequences.

? We have matrix representation of basic transformation and we can express it in the general matrix form as:

? = ?? · ? + ??

Where ? and ?′ are initial and final point position, ?? contains rotation and scaling terms and ??

contains translation al terms associated with pivot point, fixed point and reposition.

? For efficient utilization we must calculate all sequence of transformation in one step and for that reason we reformulate above equation to eliminate the matrix addition associated with translation terms in matrix ??.We can combine that thing by expanding 2X2 matrix representation into 3X3 matrices.

?It will allows us to convert all transformation into matrix multiplication but we need to represent vertex position (?, ?) with homogeneous coordinate triple (??, ??, ?) Where ? = ?? , ? = ?? thus we can also write triple as (? · ?, ? · ?, ?).

? For two dimensional geometric transformation we can take value of ? is any positive number so we can get infinite homogeneous representation for coordinate value (?, ?).

? But convenient choice is set ? = ? as it is multiplicative identity, than (?, ?) is represented as (?, ?, ?).

? Expressing coordinates in homogeneous coordinates form allows us to represent all geometric transformation equations as matrix multiplication.

? Let's see each representation with ? = ?.

Translation [?′ = ?(? ,?) · ?]

NOTE: - Inverse of translation matrix is obtain by putting −?? & − ?? instead of ?? & ??.

Rotation [?′ = ?(?) · ?]

NOTE: - Inverse of rotation matrix is obtained by replacing ? by −?.

Scaling [?′ = ?(??,??) · ?]

NOTE: - Inverse of scaling matrix is obtained by replacing ?? & ?? by ? ? & ? respectively.

<u>**Composite Transformation**</u>

? We can set up a matrix for any sequence of transformations as a composite transformation matrix by calculating the matrix product of individual transformation.

? For column matrix representation of coordinate positions, we form composite transformations by multiplying matrices in order from right to left.

Translations

? Two successive translations are performed as:

?′ = ?(???, ???) · {?(???, ???) · ?}

  ?′ = {?(???, ???) · ?(???, ???)} · ?

  ?′ = ?(??? + ???, ??? + ???) · ?}

Here ?′ and ? are column vector of final and initial point coordinate respectively

? This concept can be extended for any number of successive translations.

Rotations

? Two successive Rotations are performed as:

?′ = ?(??) · {?(??) · ?}

?′ = {?(??) · ?(??)} · ?

  ?′ = ?(?? + ??) · ?

Here ?′ and ? are column vector of final and initial point coordinate respectively.

? This concept can be extended for any number of successive rotations.

General Pivot-Point Rotation

$$\begin{bmatrix} 1 & 0 & x \\ 0 & 1 & y \\ 0 & 0 & 1 \end{bmatrix} \begin{bmatrix} \cos\theta & -\sin\theta & 0 \\ \sin\theta & \cos\theta & 0 \\ 0 & 0 & 1 \end{bmatrix} \begin{bmatrix} 1 & 0 & -x \\ 0 & 1 & -y \\ 0 & 0 & 1 \end{bmatrix}$$

$$\begin{bmatrix} \cos\theta & -\sin\theta & x(1 - \cos\theta + y\sin\theta) \\ \sin\theta & \cos\theta & y(1 - \cos\theta) - \sin\theta \\ 0 & 0 & 1 \end{bmatrix}$$

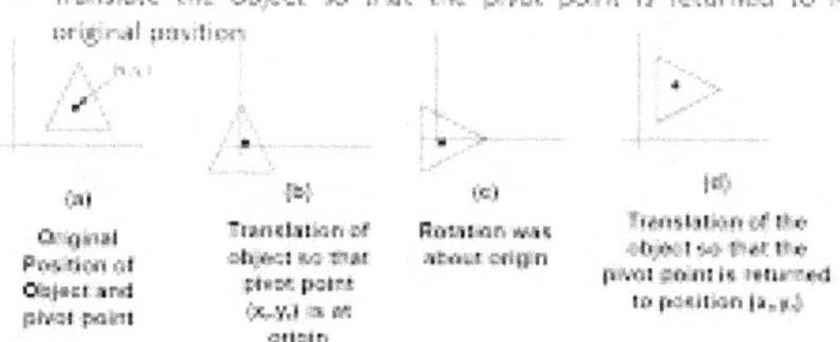

? For scaling object with position of one point called fixed point will remains same, we need to apply following sequence of transformation.

1. Translate the object so that the fixed-point coincides with the coordinate origin.

2. Scale the object with respect to the coordinate origin with specified scale factors.

3. Translate the object so that the fixed-point is returned to its original position (i.e. Inverse of step-1).

? Let's find matrix equation for this

$?' = ?(??, ??) \cdot [?(??, ??) \cdot \{?(-??, -??) \cdot ?\}]$

$?' = \{?(??, ??) \cdot ?(??, ??) \cdot ?(-??, -??)\} \cdot ?$

General Scaling Directions

? Parameter ?? and ?? scale the object along ? and ? directions. We can scale an object in other directions by rotating the object to align the desired scaling directions with the coordinate axes before applying the scaling transformation.

? Suppose we apply scaling factor ?? and ?? in direction shown in figure than we will apply following transformations.

1. Perform a rotation so that the direction for ?? and ?? coincide with ? and ? axes.

2. Scale the object with specified scale factors.

3. Perform opposite rotation to return points to their original orientations. (i.e. Inverse of step-1).

? Let's find matrix equation for this

$?' = ?{-}?(?) \cdot [?(??, ??) \cdot \{?(?) \cdot ?\}]$

$?' = \{?{-}?(?) \cdot ?(??, ??) \cdot ?(?)\} \cdot ?$

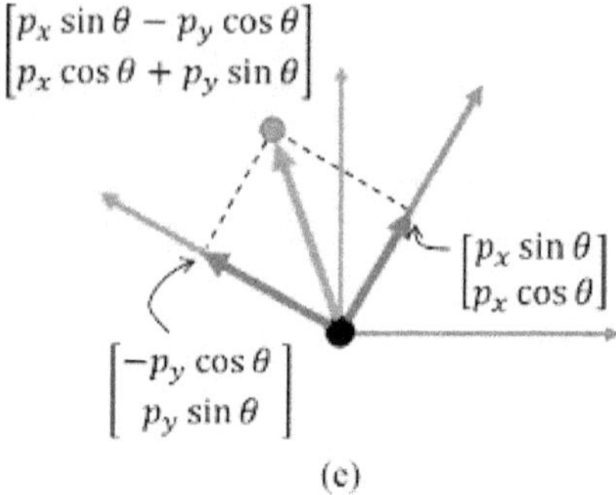

(c)

Other Transformation

? Some package provides few additional transformations which are useful in certain applications. Two such transformations are reflection and shear.

Reflection

? A reflection is a transformation that produces a mirror image of an object.

? The mirror image for a two –dimensional reflection is generated relative to an axis of reflection by rotating the object 180o about the reflection axis.

? Reflection gives image based on position of axis of reflection. Transformation matrix for few positions are discussed here.

Transformation matrix for reflection about the line $? = ?$, ??? ? ????.

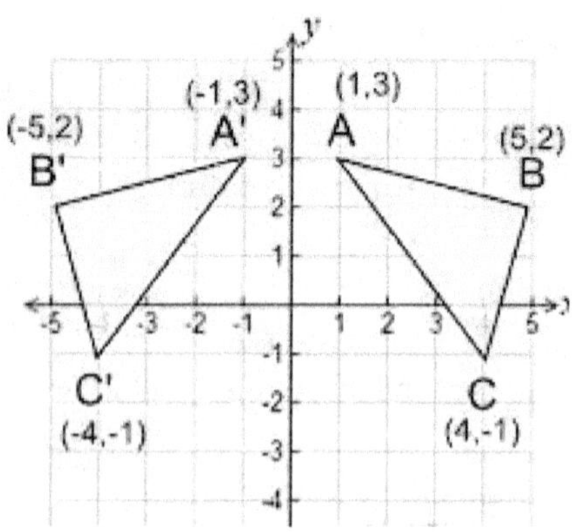

Reflection about x - axis.

? This transformation keeps x values are same, but flips (Change the sign) y values of coordinate positions.

It is a transformation which produces a mirror image of an object. The mirror image can be either about x-axis or y-axis. The object is rotated by180°.

Types of Reflection:

Reflection about the x-axis

Reflection about the y-axis

Reflection about an axis perpendicular to xy plane and passing through the origin

Reflection about line y=x

1. Reflection about x-axis: The object can be reflected about x-axis with the help of the following matrix

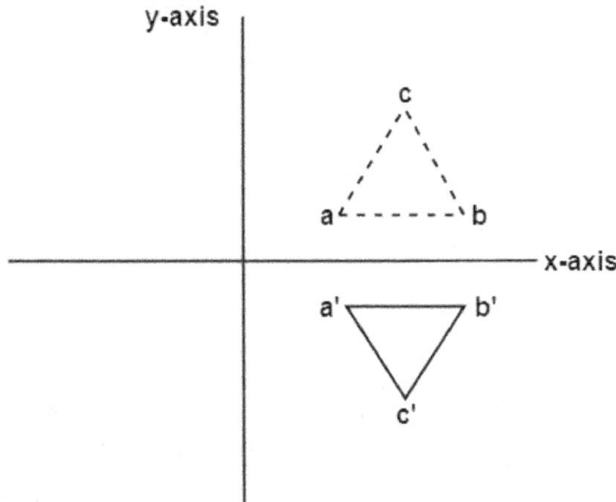

In this transformation value of x will remain same whereas the value of y will become negative.

2. Reflection about y-axis: The object can be reflected about y-axis with the help of following transformation matrix

Here the values of x will be reversed, whereas the value of y will remain the same. The object will lie another side of the y-axis.

3. Reflection about an axis perpendicular to xy plane and passing through origin:

In the matrix of this transformation is given below

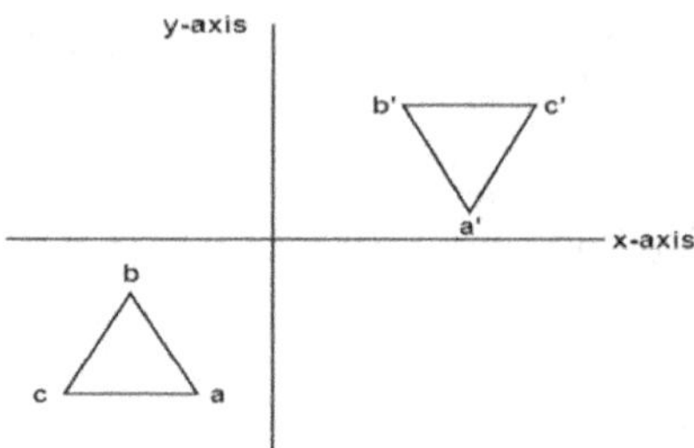

4. Reflection about line y=x: The object may be reflected about line y = x with the help of following transformation matrix

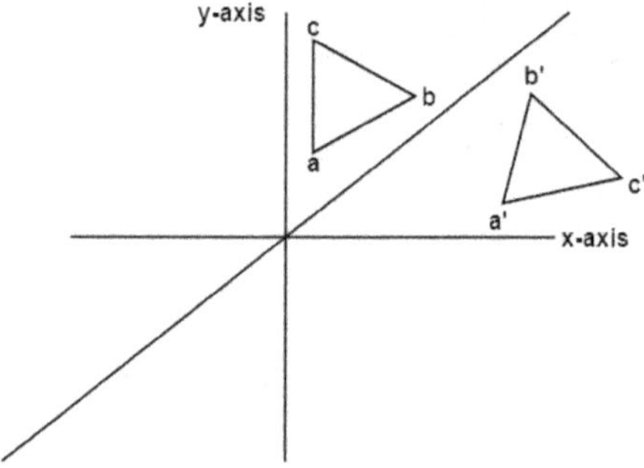

First of all, the object is rotated at 45°. The direction of rotation is clockwise. After it reflection is done concerning x-axis. The last step is the rotation of y=x back to its original position that is counterclockwise at 45°.

Program to perform Mirror Reflection about a line:.

```
#include <iostream.h>
#include <conio.h>
#include <graphics.h>
#include <math.h>
#include <stdlib.h>
#define pi 3.14
class arc
{
float x[10],y[10],theta,ref[10][10],ang;
float p[10][10],p1[10][10],x1[10],y1[10],xm,ym;
```

```cpp
int i,k,j,n;
public:
void get();
void cal ();
void map ();
void graph ();
void plot ();
void plot1();
};
void arc::get ()
{
cout<<"\n ENTER ANGLE OF LINE INCLINATION AND Y INTERCEPT";
cin>> ang >> b;
cout <<"\n ENTER NO OF VERTICES";
cin >> n;
cout <<"\n ENTER";
for (i=0; i<n; i++)
{
cout<<"\n x["<<i<<"] and y["<<i<<"]";
}
theta =(ang * pi)/ 180;
ref [0] [0] = cos (2 * theta);
ref [0] [1] = sin (2 * theta);
ref [0] [2] = -b *sin (2 * theta);
ref [1] [0] = sin (2 * theta);
ref [1] [1] = -cos (2 * theta);
ref [1] [2] = b * (cos (2 * theta)+1);
ref [2] [0]=0;
ref [2] [1]=0;
ref [2] [2] = 1;
}
void arc :: cal ()
{
for (i=0; i < n; i++)
{
p[0] [i] = x [i];
p [1] [i] = y [i];
```

```cpp
p [2] [i] = 1;
}
for (i=0; i<3;i++)
{
for (j=0; j<n; j++)
{
p1 [i] [j]=0;
for (k=0;k<3; k++)
}
p1 [i] [j] + = ref [i] [k] * p [k] [j];
}
for (i=0; i<n; i++)
{
x1 [i]=p1[0] [i];
y1 [i] = p1 [1] [i];
}
}
void arc :: map ()
{
int gd = DETECT,gm;
initgraph (&gd, &gm, " ");
int errorcode = graphresult ();
/* an error occurred */
if (errorcode ! = grOK)
{
printf ("Graphics error: %s \n", grapherrormsg (errorcode));
printf ("Press any key to halt:");
getch ();
exit (1); /* terminate with an error code */
}
}
void arc :: graph ()
{
xm=getmaxx ()/2;
ym=getmaxy ()/2;
line (xm, 0, xmm 2*ym);
}
void arc :: plot 1 ()
```

```cpp
{
for (i=0; i <n-1; i++)
{
circle (x1[i]+xm, (-y1[i]+ym), 2);
line (x1[i]+xm, (-y1[i]+ym), x1[i+1]+xm, (-y1[i+1]+ym));
}
line (x1[n-1)+xm, (-y1[n-1]+ym), x1[0]+xm, (-y1[0]+ym));
getch();
}
void arc :: plot ()
{
for (i=0; i <n-1; i++)
{
circle (x1[i]+xm, (-y1[i]+ym, 2);
line (x1[i]+xm, (-y1[i]+ym), x[i+1]+xm, (-y1[i+1]+ym));
}
line (x[n-1]+xm, (-y1[n-1]+ym), x[0]+xm, (-y[0]+ym));
getch();
}
void main ()
{
class arc a;
clrscr();
a.map();
a.graph();
a.get();
a.cal();
a.plot();
a.plot1();
getch();
}
```

CHAPTER THREE

2D VIEWING

TWO –DIMENSIONAL VIEWING

The Viewing Pipeline

? Window: Area selected in world-coordinate for display is called window. It defines what is to be viewed.

? Viewport: Area on a display device in which window image is display (mapped) is called viewport. It defines where to display.

? In many case window and viewport are rectangle, also other shape may be used as window and viewport.

? In general finding device coordinates of viewport from word coordinates of window is called as viewing transformation.

? Sometimes we consider this viewing transformation as window-to-viewport transformation but in general it involves more steps.

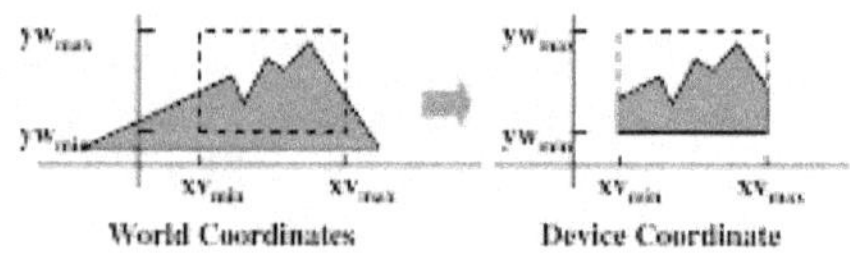

? Now we see steps involved in viewing pipeline.

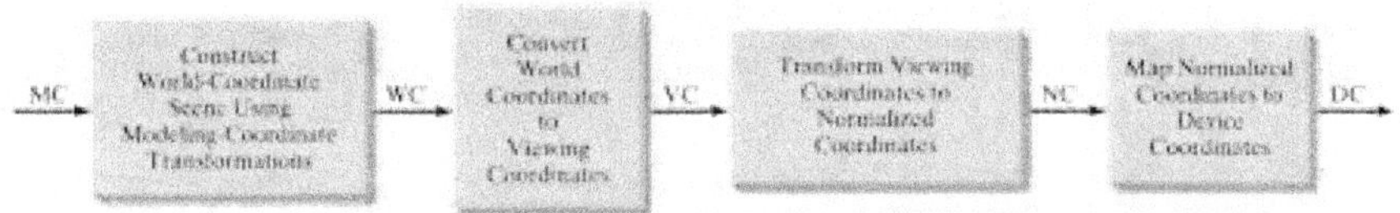

This conversation is performed with the following sequence of transformations:

- Perform a scaling transformation using a fixed point position (xwmin,ywmin) that scales the window area to the size of the viewport.
- Translate the scaled window area to the position of the viewport. Relative proportions of objects are maintained if the scaling factors are the same (sx=sy).

From normalized coordinates, object descriptions are mapped to the various display devices.

? As shown in figure above first of all we construct world coordinate scene using modeling coordinate transformation.

? After this we convert viewing coordinates from world coordinates using window to viewport transformation.

? Then we map viewing coordinate to normalized viewing coordinate in which we obtain values in between 0 to 1.

? At last we convert normalized viewing coordinate to device coordinate using device driver software which provide device specification.

? Finally device coordinate is used to display image on display screen.

? By changing the viewport position on screen we can see image at different place on the screen.

? By changing the size of the window and viewport we can obtain zoom in and zoom out effect as per requirement.

? Fixed size viewport and small size window gives zoom in effect, and fixed size viewport and larger window gives zoom out effect.

? View ports are generally defines with the unit square so that graphics package are more device independent which we call as normalized viewing coordinate.

<u>Viewing Coordinate Reference Frame</u>

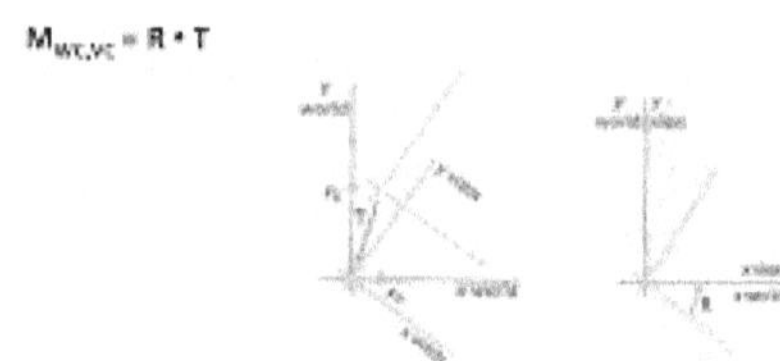

A viewing-coordinate frame is moved into coincidence with the world frame in two steps: (a) translate the viewing origin to the world origin, and then (b) rotate to align the axes of the two systems.

? We can obtain reference frame in any direction and at any position.

? For handling such condition first of all we translate reference frame origin to standard reference frame origin and then we rotate it to align it to standard axis.

? In this way we can adjust window in any reference frame.

? this is illustrate by following transformation matrix:

???,?? = ??

? Where T is translation matrix and R is rotation matrix.

<u>Window-To-Viewport Coordinate Transformation</u>

? Mapping of window coordinate to viewport is called window to viewport transformation.

? We do this using transformation that maintains relative position of window coordinate into viewport.

? That means center coordinates in window must be remains at center position in viewport.

$$\frac{xv - xv_{min}}{xv_{max} - xv_{min}} = \frac{xw - xw_{min}}{xw_{max} - xw_{min}} \quad \cdots\cdots\cdots \text{equation 1}$$

$$\frac{yv - yv_{min}}{yv_{max} - yv_{min}} = \frac{yw - yw_{min}}{yw_{max} - yw_{min}}$$

? Solving by making viewport position as subject we obtain:

$$\frac{wx - wx_{min}}{vx - vx_{min}} = \frac{wx_{max} - wx_{min}}{vx_{max} - vx_{min}} \quad and \quad \frac{wy - wy_{min}}{vy - vy_{min}} = \frac{wy_{max} - wy_{min}}{vy_{max} - vy_{min}}$$

So, solving for *vx*:

$$vx = (wx - wx_{min}) * \frac{vx_{max} - vx_{min}}{wx_{max} - wx_{min}} + vx_{min}$$

***vy* can be solved for similarly:**

$$vy = (wy - wy_{min}) * \frac{vy_{max} - vy_{min}}{wy_{max} - wy_{min}} + vy_{min}$$

? We can also map window to viewport with the set of transformation, which include following sequence of transformations:

1. Perform a scaling transformation using a fixed-point position of (xWmin,ywmin) that scales the window area to the size of the viewport.

<u>2. Translate the scaled window area to the position of the viewport.</u>

? For maintaining relative proportions we take (sx = sy). in case if both are not equal then we get stretched or contracted in either the x or y direction when displayed on the output device.

? Characters are handle in two different way one way is simply maintain relative position like other primitive and other is to maintain standard character size even though viewport size is enlarged or reduce.

? Number of display device can be used in application and for each we can use different window-to- viewport transformation. This mapping is called the workstation transformation.

Any number of output devices can we open in a particular app, and three windows to viewport transformation can be performed for each open output device.

This mapping called workstation transformation (It is accomplished by selecting a window area in normalized space and a viewport area in the coordinates of the display device).

As in fig, workstation transformation to partition a view so that different parts of normalized space can be displayed on various output devices).

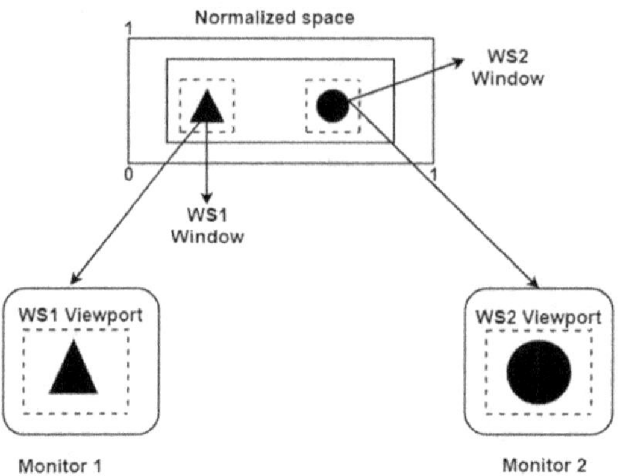

Fig:Mapping selected parts of a scene in normalized coordinates to different video monitors with workstation transformation.

Step1:Translate window to origin 1

Tx=-Xwmin Ty=-Ywmin

Step2:Scaling of the window to match its size to the viewport

Sx=(Xymax-Xvmin)/(Xwmax-Xwmin)

Sy=(Yvmax-Yvmin)/(Ywmax-Ywmin)

Step3:Again translate viewport to its correct position on screen.

Tx=Xvmin

Ty=Yvmin

Above three steps can be represented in matrix form:

VT=T * S * T1

T = Translate window to the origin

<u>Advantage of Viewing Transformation:</u>

We can display picture at device or display system according to our need and choice.

<u>Note:</u>

- World coordinate system is selected suits according to the application program.
- Screen coordinate system is chosen according to the need of design.
- Viewing transformation is selected as a bridge between the world and screen coordinate.

CHAPTER FOUR

Clipping Operations

Clipping Operations

? Generally, any procedure that identifies those portions of a picture that are either inside or outside of a specified region of space is referred to as a clipping algorithm, or simply clipping. The region against which an object is to clip is called a clip window.

? Clip window can be general polygon or it can be curved boundary.

Application of Clipping

? It can be used for displaying particular part of the picture on display screen.

? Identifying visible surface in 3D views.

? Creating objects using solid-modeling procedures.

? Displaying multiple windows on same screen.

? Drawing and painting.

It the following sections, we consider algorithms for clopping the following primitive types

i. Point Clipping

ii. Line Clipping

iii. Polygons Clipping

iv. Curve Clipping

v. Text Clipping

Point Clipping

? In point clipping we eliminate those points which are outside the clipping window and draw points which are inside the clipping window.

? Here we consider clipping window is rectangular boundary with edge (xwmin,xwmax,ywmin,ywmax).

? So for finding wether given point is inside or outside the clipping window we use following inequality:

????? ≤ ? ≤ ?????

$????? \leq ? \leq ?????$

? If above both inequality is satisfied then the point is inside otherwise the point is outside the clipping window.

Line Clipping

? Line clipping involves several possible cases.

1. Completely inside the clipping window.
2. Completely outside the clipping window.
3. Partially inside and partially outside the clipping window.

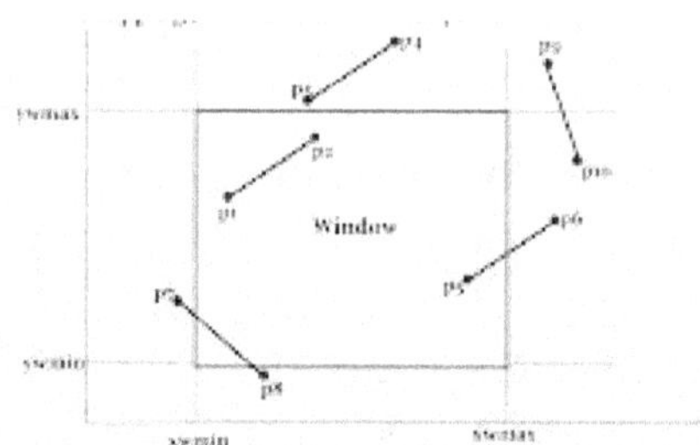

? Line which is completely inside is display completely. Line which is completely outside is eliminated from display. And for partially inside line we need to calculate intersection with window boundary and find which part is inside the clipping boundary and which part is eliminated.

? For line clipping several scientists tried different methods to solve this clipping procedure. Some of them are discuss below.

Cohen-Sutherland Line Clipping

? This is one of the oldest and most popular line-clipping procedures.

Region and Region Code

? In this we divide whole space into nine region and assign 4 bit code to each endpoint of line depending on the position where the line endpoint is located.

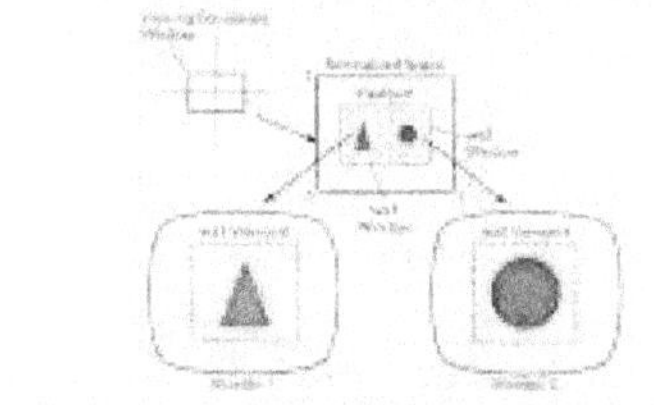

? Figure 3.6 shows code for line end point which is fall within particular area.

? Code is deriving by setting particular bit according to position of area. Set bit 1: For left side of clipping window.

Set bit 2: For right side of clipping window. Set bit 3: For below clipping window.

Set bit 4: For above clipping window.

? All bits as mention above are set means 1 and other are 0.

Liang-Barsky Line Clipping

? Line clipping approach is given by the Liang and Barsky is faster than cohen-sutherland line clipping. Which is based on analysis of the parametric equation of the line which are as below.

$? = ?? + ?\Delta?$

$? = ?? + ?\Delta?$

Where $0 \leq ? \leq 1$, $\Delta? = ?2 - ?1$ and $\Delta? = ?2 - ?1$.

Nicholl-Lee-Nicholl Line Clipping

? By creating more regions around the clip window the NLN algorithm avoids multiple clipping of an individual line segment.

? In Cohen-Sutherlan line clipping sometimes multiple calculation of intersection point of a line is done before actual window boundary intersection or line is completely rejected.

? These multiple intersection calculation is avoided in NLN line clipping procedure.

? NLN line clipping perform the fewer comparisons and divisions so it is more efficient.

? But NLN line clipping cannot be extended for three dimensions while Cohen-Sutherland and Liang-Barsky algorithm can be easily extended for three dimensions.

? For given line we find first point falls in which region out of nine region shown in figure below but three region shown in figure by putting point are only considered and if point falls in other region than we transfer that point in one of the three region.

Polygon Clipping

? For polygon clipping we need to modify the line clipping procedure because in line clipping we need to consider about only line segment while in polygon clipping we need to consider the area and the new boundary of the polygon after clipping.

Sutherland-Hodgeman Polygon Clipping

? For correctly clip a polygon we process the polygon boundary as a whole against each window edge.

? This is done by whole polygon vertices against each clip rectangle boundary one by one.

? Beginning with the initial set of polygon vertices we first clip against the left boundary and produce new sequence of vertices.

? Then that new set of vertices is clipped against the right boundary clipper, a bottom boundary clipper and a top boundary clipper, as shown in figure below.

Figure 6-19
Clipping a polygon against successive window boundaries.

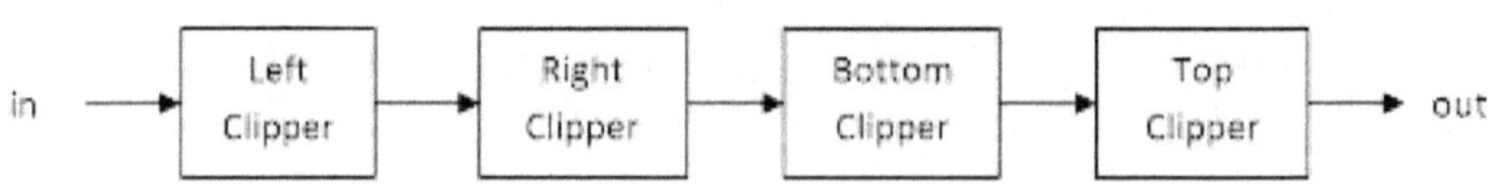

Fig. : - Processing the vertices of the polygon through boundary clipper.

? As shown in case 1: if both vertices are inside the window we add only second vertices to output list.

? In case 2: if first vertices is inside the boundary and second vertices is outside the boundary only the edge intersection with the window boundary is added to the output vertex list.

? When polygon clipping is done against one boundary then we clip against next window boundary.

? As shown in figure above we clip against left boundary vertices 1 and 2 are found to be on the outside of the boundary. Then we move to vertex 3, which is inside, we calculate the intersection and add both intersection point and vertex 3 to output list.

? Then we move to vertex 4 in which vertex 3 and 4 both are inside so we add vertex 4 to output list, similarly from 4 to 5 we add 5 to output list, then from 5 to 6 we move inside to outside so we add intersection pint to output list and finally 6 to 1 both vertex are outside the window so we does not add anything.

? Convex polygons are correctly clipped by the Sutherland-Hodgeman algorithm but concave polygons may be displayed with extraneous lines.

? For overcome this problem we have one possible solution is to divide polygon into numbers of small convex polygon and then process one by one.

? Another approach is to use Weiler-Atherton algorithm.

CURVE CLIPPING

? Curve Clipping involves complex procedures as compared to line clipping.

? Curve clipping requires more processing than for object with linear boundaries.Consider Window which is rectangular in shape.

? The circle is to consider against rectangle window. If circle is completely inside boundary of the window, it is considered visible.

? So save the circle. If a circle is in outside window, discard it. If circle cut the boundary then Consider it to be clipping case.

TEXT CLIPPING

? Several methods are available for clipping of text.

- Clipping method is dependent on the method of generation used for characters. A simple method is completely considered, or nothing considers method.

? This method is also called as all or none. If all characters of the string are inside window, then we will keep the string.

? Another method is discarded those characters not completely inside the window. If a character overlap boundary of window.

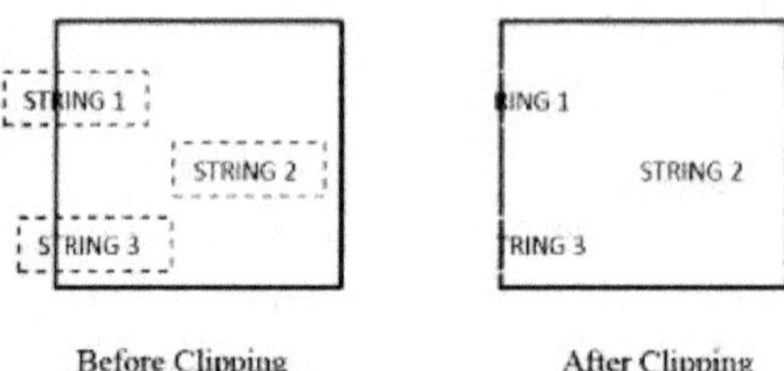

Before Clipping   After Clipping

CHAPTER FIVE

Rotate an image

Write a program to rotate an image

```c
#include<stdio.h>
#include<conio.h>
#include<math.h>
#include<process.h>
#include<graphics.h>
int x1,x2,y1,y2,mx,my,depth;
void draw();
void rotate();
void main()
{
int gd=DETECT,gm,c;
initgraph(&gd,&gm,"..s\\bgi");
printf("\n3D Transformation Rotating\n\n");
printf("\nEnter 1st top value(x1,y1):");
scanf("%d%d",&x1,&y1);
printf("Enter right bottom value(x2,y2):");
scanf("%d%d",&x2,&y2);
depth=(x2-x1)/4;
mx=(x1+x2)/2;
my=(y1+y2)/2;
draw();
getch();
cleardevice();
rotate();
getch();
}
void draw()
```

```c
{
bar3d(x1,y1,x2,y2,depth,1);
}
void rotate()
{
float t;
int a1,b1,a2,b2,dep;
printf("Enter the angle to rotate=");
scanf("%f",&t);
t=t*(3.14/180);
a1=mx+(x1-mx)*cos(t)-(y1-my)*sin(t);
a2=mx+(x2-mx)*cos(t)-(y2-my)*sin(t);
b1=my+(x1-mx)*sin(t)-(y1-my)*cos(t);
b2=my+(x2-mx)*sin(t)-(y2-my)*cos(t);
if(a2>a1)
dep=(a2-a1)/4;
else
dep=(a1-a2)/4;
bar3d(a1,b1,a2,b2,dep,1);
setcolor(5);
//draw();
}
OUTPUT:
```

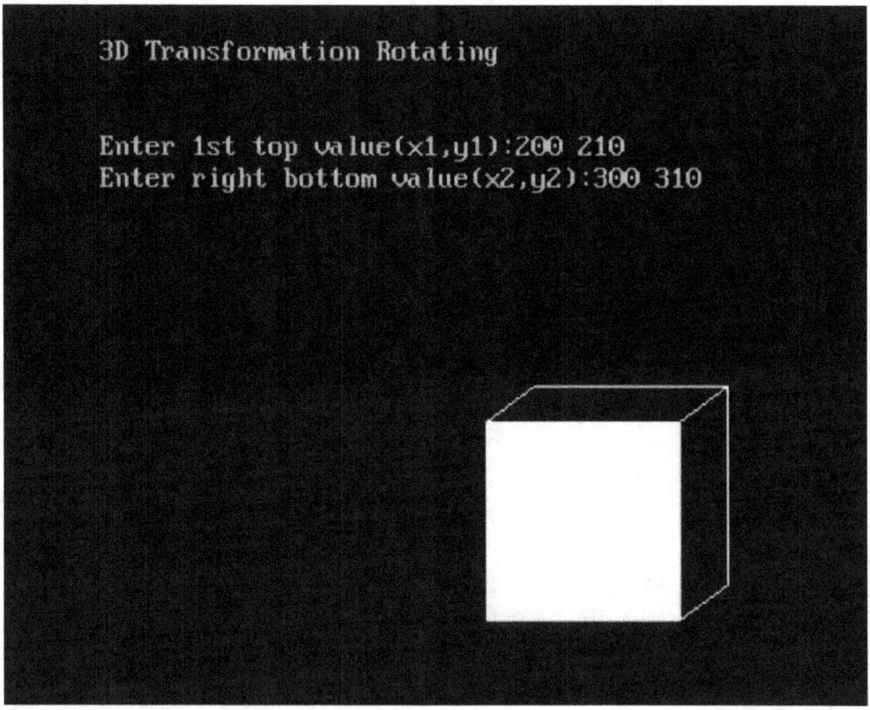

3D Transformation Rotating

Enter 1st top value(x1,y1):200 210
Enter right bottom value(x2,y2):300 310

CHAPTER SIX

DROPING WORDS

<u>Write a program to drop each word of a sentence one by one from the top</u>

```c
#include <stdio.h>
#include <stdlib.h>
#include <string.h>
int main ()
{
char str[100], word[100], twoD[10][30];
int i = 0, j = 0, k = 0, len1 = 0, len2 = 0;
printf ("Enter the string:\n");
gets (str);
printf ("Enter the word to be removed:\n");
gets (word);
// let us convert the string into 2D array
for (i = 0; str[i] != '\0'; i++)
{
if (str[i] == ' ')
{
twoD[k][j] = '\0';
k ++;
j = 0;
}
else
{
twoD[k][j] = str[i];
j ++;
}
}
twoD[k][j] = '\0';
```

```
j = 0;
for (i = 0; i < k + 1; i++)
{
if (strcmp(twoD[i], word) == 0)
{
twoD[i][j] = '\0';
}
}
j = 0;
for (i = 0; i < k + 1; i++)
{
if (twoD[i][j] == '\0')
continue;
else
printf ("%s ", twoD[i]);
}
printf ("\n");
return 0;
}
```

<u>Program Explanation</u>

1. In this C program, first step is to declare the str, word and twoD arrays. str is used to store string input, word is used to store the input word and twoD is used to store each word in 2D array.

2. Next step is to take the input from the user and also take input word that has to be removed.

3. In for loop statement, traverse until the end of the string and append the character to the n th row until you encounter a white space. If a whitespace is encountered then append \0 to the current row and iterate the steps. By the end of iterations we shall have a 2D array of words. Append \0 to the end of last row.

4. Compare the words that match the given word and make them null by using strcmp function. strcmp function is used to match two strings.

5. Print the words that are not NULL in the twoD array as output and exit.

<u>Write a program to drop each word of a sentence one by one from the top</u>

```
#include<stdio.h>
#include<conio.h>
```

```c
#include<string.h>
int main()
{
char str[100], word[20];
int i, j, ls, lw, temp, chk=0;
printf("Enter the String: ");
gets(str);
printf("Enter a Word: ");
gets(word);
ls = strlen(str);
lw = strlen(word);
for(i=0; i<ls; i++)
{
temp = i;
for(j=0; j<lw; j++)
{
if(str[i]==word[j])
i++;
}
chk = i-temp;
if(chk==lw)
{
i = temp;
for(j=i; j<(ls-lw); j++)
str[j] = str[j+lw];
ls = ls-lw;
str[j]='\0';
}
}
printf("\nNew String = %s", str);
getch();
return 0;
}
```

```
/usr/bin/ld: /tmp/ccrryons.o: In function 'main':
main.c:(.text+0x41): warning: the 'gets' function is dangerous and should not be used.
Enter the String: AISWARYAN
Enter a Word: aiswar

New String = AISWARYAN

...Program finished with exit code 0
Press ENTER to exit console.
```

drop a line using DDA Algorithm.

Write a program to drop a line using DDA Algorithm.

DDA Algorithm

DDA stands for Digital Differential Analyzer. It is an incremental method of scan conversion of line. In this method calculation is performed at each step but by using results of previous steps.

Suppose at step i, the pixels is (x_i, y_i)

The line of equation for step i

$y_i = mx_i + b$......................equation 1

Next value will be

$y_{i+1} = mx_{i+1} + b$................equation 2

$m =$

$y_{i+1} - y_i = \Delta y$......................equation 3

$y_{i+1} - x_i = \Delta x$......................equation 4

$y_{i+1} = y_i + \Delta y$

$\Delta y = m\Delta x$

$y_{i+1} = y_i + m\Delta x$

$\Delta x = \Delta y / m$

$x_{i+1} = x_i + \Delta x$

DDA Algorithm:

Step1: Start Algorithm

Step2: Declare x1,y1,x2,y2,dx,dy,x,y as integer variables.

Step3: Enter value of x1,y1,x2,y2.

Step4: Calculate dx = x2-x1

Step5: Calculate dy = y2-y1

Step6: If ABS (dx) > ABS (dy)

Then step = abs (dx)

Else
    Step7: xinc=dx/step
yinc=dy/step
assign x = x1
assign y = y1
    Step8: Set pixel (x, y)
    Step9: x = x + xinc
y = y + yinc
Set pixels (Round (x), Round (y))
    Step10: Repeat step 9 until x = x2
    Step11: End Algorithm.

```c
#include<graphics.h>
#include<conio.h>
#include<stdio.h>
void main()
{
intgd = DETECT ,gm, i;
float x, y,dx,dy,steps;
int x0, x1, y0, y1;
initgraph(&gd, &gm, "C:\\TC\\BGI");
setbkcolor(WHITE);
x0 = 100 , y0 = 200, x1 = 500, y1 = 300;
dx = (float)(x1 - x0);
dy = (float)(y1 - y0);
if(dx>=dy)
{
steps = dx;
}
else
{
steps = dy;
}
dx = dx/steps;
dy = dy/steps;
x = x0;
y = y0;
i = 1;
while(i<= steps)
```

```
{
putpixel(x, y, RED);
x += dx;
y += dy;
i=i+1;
}
getch();
closegraph();
}
```
OUTPUT:

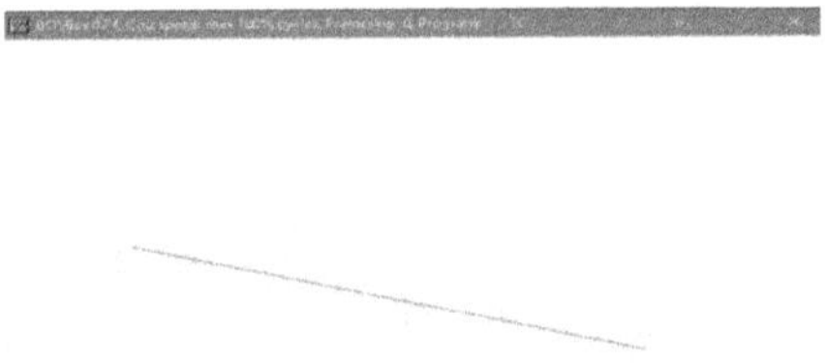

move a car with sound effect.

Write a program to move a car with sound effect.

```c
#include <stdio.h>
#include <graphics.h>
#include <conio.h>
#include <dos.h>
int main() {
int gd = DETECT, gm;
int i, maxx, midy;
/* initialize graphic mode */
initgraph(&gd, &gm, "X:\\TC\\BGI");
/* maximum pixel in horizontal axis */
maxx = getmaxx();
/* mid pixel in vertical axis */
midy = getmaxy()/2;
for (i=0; i < maxx-150; i=i+5) {
/* clears screen */
cleardevice();
/* draw a white road */
setcolor(WHITE);
line(0, midy + 37, maxx, midy + 37);
/* Draw Car */
setcolor(YELLOW);
setfillstyle(SOLID_FILL, RED);
line(i, midy + 23, i, midy);
line(i, midy, 40 + i, midy - 20);
line(40 + i, midy - 20, 80 + i, midy - 20);
line(80 + i, midy - 20, 100 + i, midy);
line(100 + i, midy, 120 + i, midy);
```

```
line(120 + i, midy, 120 + i, midy + 23);
line(0 + i, midy + 23, 18 + i, midy + 23);
arc(30 + i, midy + 23, 0, 180, 12);
line(42 + i, midy + 23, 78 + i, midy + 23);
arc(90 + i, midy + 23, 0, 180, 12);
line(102 + i, midy + 23, 120 + i, midy + 23);
line(28 + i, midy, 43 + i, midy - 15);
line(43 + i, midy - 15, 57 + i, midy - 15);
line(57 + i, midy - 15, 57 + i, midy);
line(57 + i, midy, 28 + i, midy);
line(62 + i, midy - 15, 77 + i, midy - 15);
line(77 + i, midy - 15, 92 + i, midy);
line(92 + i, midy, 62 + i, midy);
line(62 + i, midy, 62 + i, midy - 15);
floodfill(5 + i, midy + 22, YELLOW);
setcolor(BLUE);
setfillstyle(SOLID_FILL, DARKGRAY);
/* Draw Wheels */
circle(30 + i, midy + 25, 9);
circle(90 + i, midy + 25, 9);
floodfill(30 + i, midy + 25, BLUE);
floodfill(90 + i, midy + 25, BLUE);
/* Add delay of 0.1 milli seconds */
delay(100);
}
```

OUTPUT:

MOVING CAR

CHAPTER NINE

Bounce a Ball

Write a program to bounce a ball and move it with sound effect.

```c
#include <stdio.h>
#include <conio.h>
#include <graphics.h>
#include <dos.h>
int main() {
int gd = DETECT, gm;
int i, x, y, flag=0;
initgraph(&gd, &gm, "C:\\TC\\BGI");
/* get mid positions in x and y-axis */
x = getmaxx()/2;
y = 30;
while (!kbhit()) {
if(y >= getmaxy()-30 || y <= 30)
flag = !flag;
/* draws the gray board */
setcolor(RED);
setfillstyle(SOLID_FILL, RED);
circle(x, y, 30);
floodfill(x, y, RED);
/* delay for 50 milli seconds */
delay(50);
/* clears screen */
cleardevice();
if(flag){
y = y + 5;
} else {
y = y - 5;
```

```
}
}
getch();
closegraph();
return 0;
}
OUTPUT:
```

CHAPTER TEN

Pixel is Inside or Outside or on a polygon.

Write a program to test whether a given pixel is inside or outside or on a polygon.

```cpp
#include<iostream>
using namespace std;
struct Point {
int x, y;
};
struct line {
Point p1, p2;
};
bool onLine(line l1, Point p) { //check whether p is on the line or not
if(p.x <= max(l1.p1.x, l1.p2.x) && p.x <= min(l1.p1.x, l1.p2.x) &&
(p.y <= max(l1.p1.y, l1.p2.y) && p.y <= min(l1.p1.y, l1.p2.y)))
return true;
    return false;
}
    int direction(Point a, Point b, Point c) {
int val = (b.y-a.y)*(c.x-b.x)-(b.x-a.x)*(c.y-b.y);
if (val == 0)
return 0; //colinear
else if(val < 0)
return 2; //anti-clockwise direction
return 1; //clockwise direction
}
    bool isIntersect(line l1, line l2) {
//four direction for two lines and points of other line
```

```
int dir1 = direction(l1.p1, l1.p2, l2.p1);
int dir2 = direction(l1.p1, l1.p2, l2.p2);
int dir3 = direction(l2.p1, l2.p2, l1.p1);
int dir4 = direction(l2.p1, l2.p2, l1.p2);
    if(dir1 != dir2 && dir3 != dir4)
return true; //they are intersecting
if(dir1==0 && onLine(l1, l2.p1)) //when p2 of line2 are on the line1
return true;
if(dir2==0 && onLine(l1, l2.p2)) //when p1 of line2 are on the line1
return true;
if(dir3==0 && onLine(l2, l1.p1)) //when p2 of line1 are on the line2
return true;
if(dir4==0 && onLine(l2, l1.p2)) //when p1 of line1 are on the line2
return true;
return false;
}
    bool checkInside(Point poly[], int n, Point p) {
if(n < 3)
return false; //when polygon has less than 3 edge, it is not polygon
line exline = {p, {9999, p.y}}; //create a point at infinity, y is same as point
p
int count = 0;
int i = 0;
do {
line side = {poly[i], poly[(i+1)%n]}; //forming a line from two consecutive
points of poly
if(isIntersect(side, exline)) { //if side is intersects exline
if(direction(side.p1, p, side.p2) == 0)
return onLine(side, p);
count++;
}
i = (i+1)%n;
} while(i != 0);
return count&1; //when count is odd
}
    int main() {
//                        line                    polygon                    =
{{{0,0},{10,0}},{{10,0},{10,10}},{{10,10},{0,10}},{{0,10},{0,0}}};
```

```
Point polygon[] = {{0, 0}, {10, 0}, {10, 10}, {0, 10}};
Point p = {5, 3};
int n = 4;
    if(checkInside(polygon, n, p))
cout << "Point is inside.";
else
cout << "Point is outside.";
}
```